Jesse Stuart
on Education

J.R. LeMaster, Editor

THE UNIVERSITY PRESS OF KENTUCKY

Copyright © 1992 by The University Press of Kentucky

Scholarly publisher for the Commonwealth,
serving Bellarmine College, Berea College, Centre
College of Kentucky, Eastern Kentucky University,
The Filson Club, Georgetown College, Kentucky
Historical Society, Kentucky State University,
Morehead State University, Murray State University,
Northern Kentucky University, Transylvania University,
University of Kentucky, University of Louisville,
and Western Kentucky University.

Editorial and Sales Offices: Lexington, Kentucky 40508-4008

Library of Congress Cataloging-in-Publication Data

Stuart, Jesse, 1907-
Jesse Stuart on education / J.R. LeMaster, editor.

p. cm.
ISBN 0-8131-1765-8 (alk. paper)
1. Stuart, Jesse 1907–   —Biography. 2. Stuart, Jesse 1907–
—Knowledge—Education.   3. Authors, American—20th century—
Biography. 4. Education—United States—Philosophy. 5. Educators
—Kentucky—Biography. I. LeMaster, J.R., 1934–   . II. Title.
PS3537.T92516Z465   1992
371.1'0092—dc20   91-24688
[B]

This book is printed on acid-free paper meeting
the requirements of the American National Standard
for Permanence of Paper for Printed Library Materials.
∞

For E. HUDSON LONG
friend and admirer
of Jesse Stuart

Contents

Acknowledgments

Without incurring any responsibility for the ideas or information in *Jesse Stuart on Education,* various people have been both encouraging and helpful to me. I especially want to thank James M. Gifford, executive director of the Jesse Stuart Foundation, and Ann Williamson Karaffa, editor of the *Baylor Educator* and associate dean for graduate instruction in education at Baylor University, for reading my manuscript and making valuable suggestions along the way.

I am grateful to the administration at Baylor University for allowing me the time and financial support to complete this book. I am also grateful to those who allowed me to reprint selections from Jesse Stuart's work.

Introduction

EXCEPT FOR reviews, little has been written about Jesse Stuart's autobiographical books. Although the reasons for such neglect are likely numerous, two or three appear to be obvious. For example, Stuart wrote the first of these, *Beyond Dark Hills*, when he was a student at Vanderbilt University in 1932. He was born in 1906, and a rather exhaustive autobiography at the age of twenty-six seems out of keeping with the experiences and the seriousness expected of mature work in the genre. Nevertheless, *Beyond Dark Hills* contains both depth of experience and high seriousness, and it charms the reader in ways that few accounts of childhood, adolescence, and young manhood ever have.

A second reason that little has been written about the autobiographies is that they often resemble the novels, the stories, and even the poems. No clear line of demarcation seems to exist between fact and fiction. *Mr. Gallion's School* is a good example. In spite of its having been written as a novel, George Gallion is obviously Jesse Stuart. Grace is Naomi. Greenwood is Greenup, Kentucky. Kensington High School is McKell High School. Loosely, *Mr. Gallion's School* is about Stuart's returning to be principal at McKell High School following a severe heart attack in 1954. But what about the facts of *Mr. Gallion's School?* Those who subscribe to the new criticism should have little or no difficulty viewing *Mr. Gallion's School* as a novel. Those critics who do not subscribe, however, especially those who have followed Stuart's career as a writer, have a difficult time sharing that view. They will recall that he went home from Vanderbilt University in 1932 to write about his own people and that, more often than not, writing about them meant writing about himself among and interacting with them, often utilizing a first-person point of view. They will also recall how Stuart revered his land and his people as the source and substance of all his writing—a condition about which he never changed his mind.

A third reason why the autobiographies have not received the critical attention they deserve is that they focus on education more than they do any of the other genres in which the Appalachian writer worked. For many years *The Thread That Runs So True* was required or optional reading in teacher-training programs in this country and abroad, and that such was the case proved embarrassing for some academicians. How could a man who never earned a master's degree purport to tell the nation's teachers and administrators how to run their schools? Furthermore, how could the problems of a teacher in a small, rural school—and a very isolated one at that—have anything in common with the problems of a teacher in New York or Los Angeles? Despite such criticism, from the time *The Thread That Runs So True* was published in 1949 until Stuart suffered a severe stroke resulting in paralysis on 18 March 1978, he was in great demand as a speaker on education. He addressed hundreds of teachers organizations from Maine to California. He loved to lecture to teachers and administrators, for he viewed each occasion as an opportunity to do something about what he saw as the failure of our nation's schools.

On 27 March 1953, four years after publication of *The Thread That Runs So True*, Eve Blair conducted an interview with Stuart in Spartanburg, South Carolina. Ranging over a number of topics, the typescript for that interview contains an interesting statement on education:

BLAIR: Since the publication of *The Thread That Runs So True*, you have been sort of crystallized in the public mind as Mr. School Teacher of America, Jesse Stuart. We know that your ideas carry weight and your opinions will be listened to.

STUART: Well, I don't know whether I am Mr. School Teacher or not, because I borrowed so many things from so many people as I went along teaching and trying to find the way. And even when I was principal of a high school, so many of my teachers offered valuable suggestions, and we never let a teacher suggestion go by, at least I didn't. Also, when I was county superintendent, because the teaching profession is such a great one, such an important one, that we have to have all ideas.

BLAIR: What do you think of present day methods of schoolteaching, Mr. Stuart? Is there too much teaching by rote? Do you think we need more inspirational teaching of the sort you did in your little country school?

STUART: Well, I think we need inspirational teaching and we need character training for our youth in America. We need a lot of it. I may add just a simple little thing here, and it is not so simple, either, and it is not so much to the South; because, the Southerner, if he has any gift in this world and he has, many of them—he has manners. That is just natural to him. But I say in our school rooms all over America, that manners is something our students are lacking in. It is a little thing, and, yet, it's a big thing.

BLAIR: Well, Mr. Stuart, do you think that if the teachers would try to be interested in the individual pupil more—I know that they are very busy—they have too many pupils—but if they can take a personal interest, wouldn't that change the attitude of the pupil a great deal?

STUART: Yes, if a teacher would single out a student and be kind to that student, the student would be responsive. A student knows when a teacher loves him. And if the teacher says something kind to the pupil it may influence him for the rest of his life.[1]

Whether Blair's 1953 estimate of Stuart's value to American education is accurate or not, one gathers enough from his responses to the interviewer to put together a general statement about the purpose and function of education as the Kentucky educator viewed them at that time. For him, teaching was a very personal and humane activity; there could be no detachment in the classroom or out. The greatest challenge for the teacher was to inspire; learning would follow as a natural consequence. When one reads such things as "A student knows when a teacher loves him," he realizes that even in matters of education Stuart was cursed by the romantic imagination of a nineteenth-century poet. But that is the entire point, and one cannot afford to overlook it. Jesse Stuart believed in the innate goodness of man—a goodness that would be lost in the process of growing up if it was not cultivated—hence the emphasis on kindness and love. Neither should one take lightly Stuart's observation concerning manners in the South. To turn out functionally literate citizens from our schools is to do no more than half the job. The other half consists of character building. Thus the challenge to our system of education is dual by its very nature—to produce a highly literate citizenry possessed by an impeccable moral character. As far as

Jesse Stuart was concerned in 1953, the future of our civilization depended on meeting this challenge, and it still does.

The selections in this collection are taken from *Beyond Dark Hills* (1938), *The Thread That Runs So True* (1949), *The Year of My Rebirth* (1956), *God's Oddling* (1960), *Mr. Gallion's School* (1967), and *To Teach, To Love* (1970). The last of the autobiographies, *The Kingdom Within* (1979), is not represented because it contributes little to the scope of this collection—to present the reader with a loosely chronological record of Jesse Stuart's experiences as a student and as an educator.[2] The university years have been slighted and could very well form the substance of another collection. Because his experiences as teacher and administrator were confined largely to elementary and secondary schools, it seemed appropriate that this collection focus on those years: on Stuart as preschool and school child as well as on Stuart as teacher and administrator. In these selections, nonetheless, whether he assumes a fictitious name or not, the point of view is that of Stuart. He is telling his own story—often with a great amount of tenderness toward those who taught him and a great amount of love for the hundreds of his former students who are scattered about the world.

The first of the selections, "Early Education," taken from *God's Oddling*, is a tribute to Stuart's father. Published twenty-two years after *Beyond Dark Hills*, it contains a retelling of some material from the earlier work, material that acquires a new significance in its new context. The chronology, therefore, is in the telling rather than in the publication dates of the autobiographies.

One should not be confused by the fact that *God's Oddling* is a tribute to Stuart's father, who never learned to read or write. His father was a remarkable educator, as the son tells us, a born teacher who inspired his children to work, to dream, and to look for beauty in the simplest of things: "My father didn't have to travel over the country searching for something beautiful to see. He didn't have to go away to find beauty, for he found it everywhere around him. He had eyes to find it. He had a mind to know it. He had a heart to appreciate it. He was an uneducated poet of this earth. And if anybody had told him that he was, he wouldn't have understood. He would have turned and walked away without saying anything."[3]

Jesse Stuart's father was his first and greatest teacher. The two of them spent many pleasurable times in the fields and woods identifying and observing flora and fauna. Finding a rare wild flower became a game, and young Jesse loved it. Cutting corn became a game, and he loved that too. After supper, the Stuart family would sit at the table for hours telling stories and playing games: "We went to our supper table hungry and we came away happy, full of food and great dreams." Later, when he became a teacher, Stuart would not forget the pleasure he had experienced as a child who was learning, and that learning should be fun became a major premise in his mature philosophy of education. Most importantly, young Jesse's father always encouraged his son to get an education and amount to something. When Jesse was three years old, his father carried him three miles to show him a schoolhouse. He writes of his father, "Pa talked to me about getting an education from the time I can remember. Winter evenings he'd talk to me about going to school to learn to read and write. When I'd ride behind him on the mule, with my arms around his waist, he'd talk about how hard life would be for me if I didn't know how to read and write."

"Beyond Dark Hills," the selection taken from his first autobiographical book, contains a record of Stuart's high school days. In it he tells how he traveled to the city of Greenup for work, and how while he was working on a concrete mixer he discovered Greenup High School: "When I saw that schoolhouse I had many thoughts. I would go home and get my sister and we would come to this place to school." He did not find the school work hard, but he had a difficult time socially. His clothes made him extremely self-conscious, and he ate his lunches in seclusion: "When I ate my lunch that I brought wrapped in a newspaper, I always got away from the other boys. I went around by the old flour mills. I didn't want them to see biscuits with meat and mustard between, and the cornbread."

In the book *Beyond Dark Hills* the reader witnesses the shaping of a young man's sensibility—the real beginning of a writer's sensibility as well as that of a fine teacher. Stuart tells how he spent the summer after his freshman year at Fort Knox, where he was tossed in a blanket because he did not conform. His sophomore year, he writes, was a happy time for him. He hewed crossties and sold them to buy clothes. He took his hound, his lantern, and his books and went into the hills at night. Of those times he writes, "There was loneliness in the dark hills when the wind stirred the withered leaves on the trees. It was music to me. It was poetry. It hangs to me better than a piece of clothing for it fits me well and will not wear out." This was the year he began to write poetry, and his first year to study literature in school. Stuart fell in love with literature. Evenings he would go home and steal quietly into the woods to write. It was also the time in which he began to philosophize about life and any meaning it might have.

After his sophomore year he took a supply of poetry by Tennyson and Burns and went off to live in a cave. He loved the isolation. After his junior year he took a teacher's examination and earned his second-class certificate, after which he went out and taught in a country school for a year. Of his first student he writes, "It took play and association to make them keen and alert as well as it took books. They were starved for association." He returned to high school with confidence and completed his senior year only to confront the problem of what to do with his future.

In "The Thread That Runs So True," the third selection, Stuart writes of his returning home from Lincoln Memorial University, after having been away for three years, determined to return to his work in a steel mill. As he explains, five years had passed since he last taught school. Although he had taken no courses in education to prepare himself for teaching, he once again ended up in an isolated backwoods school. He taught fourteen students in a "squat, ugly little structure" that had been used as a lodge. As it turned out, his problem, he contends, was "keeping ahead of these pupils." His students were exceptionally bright and eager to learn, although none of their parents were high school graduates. Stuart built an entire system of learning around the idea of recreation. He fished, hunted, and skated with his students. He devised numerous games for indoor recreation during the winter months. He fell in love with teaching and waxed very philosophical about it:

I thought if every teacher in every school in America—rural, village, city, township, church, public, or private—could inspire his pupils with all the power he had, if he could teach them as they had never been taught before to live, to work, to play, and to share, if he could put ambition into their brains and hearts, that would be a great way to make a generation of the greatest citizenry America had ever had. All of this had to begin with the little unit. Each teacher had to do his share. Each teacher was responsible for the destiny of America, because the pupils came under his influence. The teacher held the destiny of a great country in his hand as no member of any other profession could hold it. All other professions stemmed from the products of his profession.

Within this great profession, I thought, lay the solution of most of the cities', counties', states', and the nation's troubles. It was within the teacher's province to solve most of these things. He could put inspiration in the hearts and brains of his pupils to do greater things upon this earth. The schoolroom was the gateway to all the problems of humanity. It was the gateway to the correcting of evils. It was the gateway to inspire the nation's succeeding generations to greater and more beautiful living with each other; to happiness, to health, to brotherhood, to everything!

I thought these things as I walked in the somber autumn beside this river [the Tiber] and watched the leaves fall from the tall bankside trees to the blue swirling water. And I believed deep in my heart that I was a member of the greatest profession of mankind.

The students at Winston High School accomplished remarkable things, and Stuart became a remarkable teacher, but at the end of the year he left to become principal of Landsburgh (Greenup) High School, which he had entered several years before as a student with only thirty months of rural schooling.

To Teach, To Love was criticized for being disjointed when it appeared in 1970. Containing a considerable amount of previously published material, it lacked the narrative quality that had characterized Stuart's writing to that time. The selection included here is typical, but it is also valuable because in it the writer discusses pedagogy.

Having been a teacher, a principal, and a superintendent, Stuart decided that he needed more knowledge to meet the educational challenges of his time. He enrolled at George Peabody College, where his teachers, he writes, were "educational giants." He studied philosophy of education under Dr. Alfred Leland Crabb, for whom he wrote a paper entitled "Uncle Mel," a paper on the philosophy of his uncle Martin Hilton. Deeply concerned about the economic and social plight of the American teacher, Stuart traveled to Europe on a Guggenheim fellowship. He visited schools in Denmark, Norway, Sweden, Finland, Estonia, Latvia, Lithuania, Poland, Holland, Belgium, France, Switzerland, and Czechoslovakia. In every country, he found, teachers were paid relatively well and enjoyed a level of social status unknown by teachers in America.

In this selection from *To Teach, To Love* Stuart discusses how he taught his students to write, how he taught the short story, how he created interest in the classroom, and how he handled discipline. As a teacher he never forgot the enjoyment he'd had as a child under the tutelage of his father, which he discusses at some length. The selection contains an account of his teaching his young daughter in the same way that his father taught him. It ends with his returning to McKell High School as principal in 1956, two years after an almost-fatal heart attack.

"Remembering Teachers" contains a series of tributes to teachers from *The Year of My Rebirth*, written while Stuart was recuperating from the heart attack he had in 1954. He wrote extensively about his teachers and about the schools he attended. He often found much to praise, and he never tired of expressing his gratitude for those teachers who took an interest in him. In "Remembering Teachers" he pays tribute to Calvin Clarke: "Naomi had dinner ready and waiting. My mind went back through the years as I watched eagerly for him. I had known C.C. since 1912. He was my first teacher, and he became my friend for life. It was he who taught me to read and write. How could I ever forget him? My father was the district school trustee at Plum Grove then. He recommended this small, slender eighteen-year old high school graduate. Little did we children know then that we were going to school to a man who would create a legend some day." Stuart spends much time articulating the legend of his first teacher, a success story very like his own. Clarke died on 4 January 1960, and until his death he successfully managed Stuart's financial affairs.

He next pays tribute to Mrs. Robert Hatton, a high school English teacher who introduced him to the poetry of Robert Burns. Burns changed his life, he contends: "If this man, Robert Burns, a Scottish plowboy who was born in a poor home and never had many opportunities, could grow up to write poetry that would endure, why can't I? I am of Scottish descent. I was born in a one-room shack in the Kentucky hills, and I, too, plow the soil. Why can't I do it if Burns could?" He imaginatively transformed his Kentucky hills into Burns's beloved Scotland. "Robert Burns was within my reach," he writes. "We were born under the same circumstances." He loved Mrs. Hatton because she took an interest in him, because she would sit and discuss Burns with him, and because she inspired him to strive for accomplishment, for greatness.

He also writes of Lena Wells Lykins Voiers, who came from sturdy pioneer stock: "As I walked the ridge path with Lena Wells that January afternoon thirty-three years ago, when she was twenty-six and I was fifteen, she told me that I would write a book someday if I worked hard enough. And she told me that she would always keep in touch with me. That moment I had my first stirrings of ambition to try to amount to something in life, simply because she had so much confidence in me. But I thought when I left Greenup High School and she went back to her home town, Vanceburg, that we would not see each other again." He pays tribute to Harry Harrison Kroll, his first college English teacher, and to Donald Davidson, under whom he studied at Vanderbilt University. They also encouraged and inspired him, and he fondly held them in his memory as models for what a great teacher should be.

The last selection, "The School Bell Rings Again," is taken from *Mr. Gallion's School,* which is generally considered inferior to Stuart's earlier work. It relates the story of his decision to return to McKell High School as principal two years after the 1954 heart attack. Set in a barbershop in Greenup, it consists of a dialogue among interested parents and townspeople about how Kensington (McKell) High School had declined and was in need of a strong administrator. George Gallion (Stuart) assesses the situation, not knowing that the chairman of the local board of education is listening attentively. When he is approached by the chairman of the board, Gallion remarks, "I've got a doctor and a wife who'll have to pass on me, . . . Each has a vote, and I'll have one." Gallion's wife, Grace, protests bitterly, but his doctor approves, and he happily returns to what he calls a "headquarters of educational enlightenment for thousands of young Americans," even though the building is terribly dilapidated and run down.

Stuart died on 17 February 1984. He will never again travel across America lecturing to thousands of teachers and administrators. The voice of Jesse Stuart is still needed, however, and perhaps now more than ever before. In an age of pessimism concerning our schools, his philosophy of optimism is needed. His unwavering belief in the value of educating all Americans is needed. His challenge to teachers to walk proudly because they belong to the greatest profession in the world is needed. His unbounded confidence in the potential of America's young people is needed.[4]

Yes, we need the voice and vision of Jesse Stuart. How will we solve the problems of loneliness, teenage pregnancy, drug addiction, alcoholism, and—perhaps most frightening—functional illiteracy that plague our schools? We will not do it by using giant corporations as our model, for they are committed to a philosophy of consumerism. Furthermore, to rationalize that the problems in our schools are symptomatic of the sickness of our society in general will solve neither the problems of the schools nor those of the society. Perhaps what we need is a bold, new attempt to examine what it means to be human in our time, and in conducting such an examination honestly, we may very well discover what it has meant to be human all along. In the final analysis, education is not merely education. It supposes a future in which someone is becoming—is imagining what it is like to be—more human, and in doing so provides hope and direction for those who come later.

Notes

1. Unpublished interview, conducted by Eve Blair at Spartanburg, South Carolina, 27 March 1953. Found in the vertical file at Murray State University Library, Murray, Kentucky.

2. Also excluded is *Cradle of the Copperheads* (New York: McGraw-Hill, 1988), edited by Paul Douglass and published four years after Stuart's demise, which is more about the politics of education than about education itself. Specifically, it is a fictionalized account of Stuart's experience as superintendent of Greenup County Schools.

3. This and all further quotations are taken from the selections being discussed.

4. Recent studies on the failure of our nation's schools include E.D. Hirsch, Jr., *Cultural Literacy* (Boston: Houghton Mifflin, 1987), and Allan Bloom, *The Closing of the American Mind* (New York: Simon and Schuster, 1987). Hirsch argues that for the past fifty years our theories of educa-

tion—based mostly on Jean Jacques Rousseau's ideas about education as natural development—have been wrong. Hirsch offers an alternative in the form of a corrective theory, which turns out to be an anthropological approach to education. Cultural memory has deteriorated, contends Hirsch, because we have mistakenly emphasized the learning of basic communication skills over the learning of content. Therefore, the way out of our dilemma, according to Hirsch, lies in teaching the information necessary for succeeding in our world.

Bloom, on the other hand, strikes out at reductionism, pluralism, value relativism, and in general the absurdities that have come to characterize our lives both in and out of school. Bloom agrees with Hirsch that man is more a cultural than a natural being, but any similarity between the two largely ends there. Believing acceptable solutions cannot be found in a world where *values* replace good and evil, Bloom moves back through time in search of a model for our schools and locates it in ancient philosophical and literary texts which have always taught the value of self-knowledge—that knowledge having to do with man and his place in the universe.

After reading Hirsch and Bloom, one comes away with an appreciation for Jesse Stuart—with an appreciation for his conviction that if we bring the usable past to bear upon the moment we will teach both how to live and how to make a living. After all, our interest does not ultimately lie in theories, but in how we live our lives.

Early Education

WHEN *God's Oddling* was published in 1960, reviews were both plentiful and favorable. Donald L. Ball described it as an engaging and moving story with charm and sincerity (*Richmond Times-Dispatch*, 20 November 1960), and Van Allen Bradley saw it as a memorable portrait written in human terms (*Chicago Daily News*, 24 December 1960). Fanny Butcher saw in *God's Oddling* a true poet of the soil (*Chicago Tribune*, 20 November 1960), and Roland Carter was pleased with Stuart's message of genuine family love (*Chattanooga Daily Times*, 4 December 1960). John Goodspeed described the book as occasionally repetitious but one of Stuart's best (*Baltimore Sun*, 25 December 1960), and William J. Griffin saw it as a case of complexity disguised as simplicity (*Nashville Banner*, 16 December 1960). Other reviewers called it tribute, lamentation, and memorial. Frederick H. Guidry suggested that Stuart sometimes confused fact and fiction, but he liked the writer's tribute to decency and affection (*Christian Science Monitor*, 10 November 1960). Anne Pence Davis likened the work to a patchwork quilt in that it was pieced together from previously published materials (*Oklahoma City Daily Oklahoman*, 27 November 1960), but all in all the reviewers agreed with Ted Pfeiffer, who viewed the book as a loving tribute that could not have been written by anyone other than a poet (*Louisville Times*, 8 November 1960).

Anna Pence Davis was right in observing that the book was put together with previously published pieces. No fewer than ten pieces, published in the 1930s, 1940s, and 1950s, were written into the text, but that in no way tells the complete story. In a brief preface at the beginning of the book, Stuart explains: "This is the one book I have wanted most to write all my life. It is about my father, Mitchell Stuart. It is for him, too. Even though my father was unable to read or write anything but his own name, I believe he was a great man. He was great in spirit and great in his influence upon others. There is no other man I have ever loved or respected more. When I set out to write this book, I discovered that I had already been writing it all my life, for I had written poems and stories and articles about my father from the time I started writing. *God's Oddling*, then, is the harvest of all my writing seasons. It is the best book I could write, and I hope it is worthy of the man I have tried to portray." Stuart goes on to explain the use of "oddling" in the title and makes reference to his father's death, the impact of which profoundly affected him, as indicated by the last paragraph of the book: "Knowing he is dead and buried, I still find it hard to believe he is gone. This is why I think I hear him when it is only the wind in the willow leaves. I think I hear his hoe turning the stones over again in his corn row. How can he leave this world where his image is stamped so indelibly upon everything? He is still a part of this valley, just as it is still a part of him."

On Mother's Day of 1951 he had buried his mother in Plum Grove Cemetery, and as H. Edward Richardson writes in *Jesse* (New York: McGraw-Hill, 1984), "All his achievements in 1951 were starkly overshadowed by a profound sadness that was never wholly to leave him" (341). The sadness was more than compounded upon the death of his father on 23 December 1954. On 8 October of the same year Stuart had suffered an almost-fatal heart attack in Murray, Kentucky. About the death of Stuart's father, Richardson writes, "That October of 1954 a darkness had closed in upon his life. Now in December, another dark, a dark within the darkness, had fallen, too, and there was no deeper darkness than this valley. Yet for now he must, crippled heart and all, walk through the valley of the shadow" (359).

The following selection from *God's Oddling*, which is a record of Stuart's early education, is included here because it is all memory. It is a record of the writer's memories of how his father taught and inspired a young boy to love the earth and all that is on it. As his old friend and teacher, Donald Davidson, wrote in a letter to Stuart, "Jesse, remember, that though you have personally lost a father in the way of mortality no human being can escape in the flesh, you have made his mortality into immortality in your poems and your prose where he lives and will live for all the world" (Richardson, 396). Here we have the flesh made spirit.

Here more than anywhere else we have Jesse Stuart immortalized through what he would make immortal in a man's images of a small boy who idolized his father.

During my childhood, when the supper bell rang, we didn't waste any time getting to the house. This was the greatest time of day for everybody. If we were doing some little job, we dropped our tools and hurried to the house. If we were feeding the livestock, we rushed our work. This was the time when each member of the family reported to the others what he had done that day and made his plans for the next. It is hard for me to remember when our suppertime lasted only an hour. We used to sit around the table for as long as three hours after we had eaten.

Back when I had only a brother and an older sister, Mom cooked on a big flat-topped stove in the corner of our kitchen. After supper Pa would sit at the table and tell us how his father took leases up Big Sandy and cleared as much as twenty acres of ground the first year. He told us how his father split the chestnuts, fenced the clearing with rails, plowed the land with cattle, sowed some of it in wheat, and planted the rest in corn the first year. That was a lot of ground to clear of saw-log timbers, but there were a lot of Stuarts. My father was the youngest of eleven children, and all the boys, and girls too, worked in the fields. He told us of the great crops Grandpa had grown, how rich the soil had been for three or four years, and what handsome rail fences he had made. He told us how the neighbors would set the woods on fire in the spring to kill the copperheads, and how fire under the rail fences around the clearings had left charred embers. This part of his story would make me tense and upset. I never wanted the rail fences to burn.

Mom told us stories of her father back in Carter County, who had once cut a hundred twenty shocks of corn, twelve hills square, in a day. He tied a middle band in the shock and two on the outside. Once he lifted a rock into a wagon bed that was so large it went through the floor. In those days they had few books and no magazines and newspapers to read in this part of the country, and the winter months in a small cabin, especially when snow or thaw isolated them, could be pretty trying. They would pop corn and roast potatoes in the ashes and tell tales over and over until people got tired of hearing them. But all these stories, repeated to us at suppertime, seemed fascinating. I wanted them to go on and on. I couldn't wait to finish eating and then hear our parents talk of long ago.

After my sister and I started to school, we had something to talk about at the supper table. If I had been wild at school and got switched, Sophia couldn't wait to get to the supper table to tell it. But if I got a headmark and turned Carrie Burkhardt down in spelling, I couldn't wait to tell it. If I won in an arithmetic match, I never stopped talking about it at supper. We told Pa and Mom about everything we had seen on our way to and from school. Our parents were good listeners as well as good talkers. At suppertime in this three-room house a family tradition of swapping the day's doings started.

One of my father's favorite games was to take a different farm each evening and tell us what he would do to improve the place if he were only able to buy it. By the rules of this game, we owned every farm we had ever rented, and where we lived now made six, plus a lot of other farms where we hadn't lived but had rented patches on the shares. My father would tell where he would make meadows, have pastures, build a house, set an orchard, the woods he'd leave for timber and the fields he would clear and sow for pasture. When he got through telling about these farms, not only were they beautiful and vastly improved but we owned them. We went to our supper table hungry and we came away happy, full of food and great dreams.

When we moved on to a new place, our seventh rented farm, we didn't have as much food to set on the supper table because the thin, sandy soil wouldn't produce it. A sister was born here, and my father now had a family of seven to feed. We didn't have too much to eat, but we still had fun at the supper table. This was when we started joking about the bumblebee corn we had raised, where the bee sat on the corn tassel sucking nectar while his wing tips rested on the ground. And at hog-killing time in October, we talked about how our hogs were so large and fat we'd hang four of them on the clothesline. We kidded about the washtubs being too close to the clothesline, for a hog might fall off the line into the tub and we'd lose him. Sometimes this talk at the supper table brought Pa up from his chair. He tried to turn the subject by telling us how many cattle he had broken to plow and how much money he would make breaking cattle. But we kept on talking about porkers hanging on the clothesline and about bumblebee corn because we didn't know it was hurting Pa's feelings.

I remember now the Christmases of my childhood. Not the Christmases of December 25 that we know, but the Old Christmas that came on January 7.

If Mom and Pa believed Christ was born on January 7, then we believed it, too. We had faith in their wisdom and goodness. But our main concern was that people should not stop celebrating both the first and the second Christmas. It was like having two birthday celebrations every year. It wasn't until years later, in college, that I understood that the January 6-7 date was that of the Epiphany celebrated by the Eastern Church and that it had taken those twelve days between December 25 and January 6 for the Wise Men to follow the star to Bethlehem.

Our mother and father told us that on January 7 the violets bloomed again under last year's leaves and the snow. They told us that the mountain daisy and often the apple, peach, and pear would bloom. When I was a child, I searched for proof of these things. I don't remember ever finding proof. But later, whenever apple, peach, pear, and daisy bloomed early, I remembered about the legend of January 7. Often I have found violets blooming under last year's leaves and under the snow, but never as early as January 7. I wanted to believe this legend because I thought it a beautiful idea. Because of these stories, Old Christmas was the one I preferred.

My mother and father said that the fox wouldn't catch the birds and the dog wouldn't harm the rabbits on Old Christmas. They quoted the Bible where the lamb and the lion lay down together. They told us God created all these animals and that they were kind to each other on this night of the Saviour's birth. I always wanted to see a fox and a covey of quail lie down together. I wanted to see what would happen.

Another beautiful legend of love had it that on this night all animals could speak to each other in the same language and understand each other. The owl respected the pheasant while the chicken hawk spoke to the chickadee, wren, and ground sparrow. The weak had a voice equal to that of the strong. I felt closer to this Christmas because of the special respect the animals and birds paid the birth of our Saviour.

On both Christmas Days my father always gave his livestock extra rations of feed. He put extra ears of corn in the feeding boxes for our horses or mules, and he gave our cows more cracked corn or soft corn nubbins. He gave our cattle extra hay, and he fed our swine more warm gruel made of ground corn and food scraps mixed up in warm water. We never, at Christmas or any other time, gave our hogs swill, which we regarded as unclean.

We children used to wonder in what language the animals spoke to each other and what they said. We often wished that Christ had made it possible for them to have been friendlier with each other all year round, especially when we would find a rabbit's blood frozen on the snow on our way to Plum Grove School where a fox had made off with him in the night. My older sister, Sophia, and I used to wonder if animals went to our Heaven or if they went to a Heaven for their own kind or if they went to a Heaven for all the animals and birds. If they went to our Heaven and we had killed them on earth, what would we say to them there? I had these thoughts.

Perhaps I had these thoughts because for so many months of the year we were completely isolated from the rest of the world, isolated within our own world and our own thoughts. We had no roads, and when it snowed we were cut off and alone. Wherever the hard-roads ran, which we called winter roads then, isolation disappeared. These hard-roads became winter lifelines.

We never got a winter road here until after World War II. However, we had made strides against isolation. We had an automobile. We built a road ourselves. We put up bridges (which the heavy trucks later smashed) so that we could get over the streams when they were full. But we often had to drive through mudholes, almost swimming our car through the mud, in the early forties. We read the skies and winds the best we could before we drove our car out, but often we fell short of perfection as weather prophets.

Members of my family remember further back, when the only ways we had of getting out of this landlocked valley were to walk or to ride a horse or mule. I myself remember the days when snow lay on the ground from November until March, and we children lived in a small landlocked world with no books, victrolas, or radios to amuse us. We didn't get a paper or a magazine and had to depend on our own imaginations and what nature provided for our entertainment. I sometimes think that this taught us to be resourceful. We made up some wild and fanciful games then.

By our winter road, we are less than ten minutes from Greenup today. When I used to drive our team of horses over the almost impassable roads, through holes where the high axles dragged, it took me a half day to get to Greenup and back if I was lucky. This was a long half day and took so much freshness from the team when we got there and back the same day. I seldom made the return trip the same day. If I did, I would still be traveling at nightfall on this short winter day, and I would hang a lantern on one of my horses to light our way up the dark valley.

Those were the days when my father claimed that a circle around the moon meant bad weather within three days. If the circle was unusually bright, this meant rough weather within a week. When we heard a lonesome steamboat whistle from over the high hills and down in the valley of the Ohio River or the steam-locomotive whistles on the Kentucky and the Ohio sides of the river, distances of six and eight miles away, we knew to prepare for a siege of rough winter. We would bring a load of necessary supplies from Greenup in a hurry, carrying them on horseback or walking them home in a basket.

Red skies in the morning were a warning, too, as were the soft breaths of wind that swept intermittently up the valley. When the mules and horses ran in the pasture, kicked up their heels, and rode each other, this was a sign. When wild rabbits ate the sassafras bark up ten, fifteen, or twenty inches high, we looked for a snow that deep, and when the owls hooted lonesome-like in the afternoon, we looked for stormy weather. There were so many signs that my father used. He would have no truck with what he called "those hit-and-miss calendars and almanacs." We had our own set of rules, and we were our own prophets. Accurate or not, our way was more fun than listening to weather forecasts from a radio beside our breakfast table.

Our isolation had its charms. We used to watch the blooms in spring on the wild raspberry, blackberry, dewberry, strawberry, service tree, and wild crab apples to see how heavy their crops might be. And we watched frosts later, and often went to the plum, peach, and apple trees to see if a frost or a near freeze had damaged the fruit.

Yes, we lived by signs or what people now would call super-stitions. When I was old enough to learn anything, I learned to respect the pewees. My father and mother loved those birds. And, in the little house where I lived until I was nine, a pair came each spring. My father used to say, "Must be time to plow the garden, our pewees are back." Nothing, no sign or indication, escaped my father. I recall he always told me to expect rain when the leaves spiraled up toward the sky, and so whenever I see oak leaves twisting up from the strong, sturdy boughs, turning over and showing their soapy bellies to the wind and hot sun, I know that a storm is coming and I remember my father.

Nothing ever escaped my father for he was an earth poet who loved the land and everything on it. He liked to watch things grow. From the time I was big enough for him to lead me by the hand, I went with him over the farm. If I couldn't walk all the way in those early days, he'd carry me on his back. I learned to love many of the things he loved.

I went with my father to so many fields over the years and listened to him talk so often about their beauty that I know now that he had wonderful thoughts which should have been written down. Thoughts came to him faster than a hummingbird flits from one blossom to another.

Sometime in the dim past of my boyhood, my father unloaded me from his back under some white-oak trees just beginning to leaf. "Look at this hill, son," he said, gesturing broadly with a sweep of his hand. "Look up that steep hill toward the sky. See how pretty that new-ground corn is."

This was the first field I can remember my father's taking me to see. The rows of corn curved like dark-green rainbows around a high slope with a valley and its little tributaries running down through the center. The corn blades rustled in the wind, and my father said he could understand what the corn blades were say-ing. He told me they whispered to each other, and this was hard for me to believe. I reasoned that before anything could speak or make a sound it had to have a mouth. When my father said the corn could talk, I got down on my knees and I looked a stalk over.

"This corn hasn't got a mouth," I told my father. "How can anything talk when it doesn't have a mouth?"

He laughed like the wind in the corn and hugged me to his knees, and we went on.

On a Sunday, when my mother and sisters were at church, my father took me by the hand and led me across two valleys to a cove where once giant beech timber had stood. He was always restless on Sundays, eager to get back to the fields in which he worked all week. He had cleared a piece of this land to raise white corn, which he planned to have ground for meal to make our bread. He thought this cove was suited to white corn. He called it Johnson County corn. Someone had brought the seed from the Big Sandy River, in the county where my father was born and lived until he was sixteen. When he had cleared this cove, set fire to the giant beech tops, and left ash over the new ground, he thought this earth would produce cornfield beans too. In every other hill of corn he had planted beans. Now these beans ran up the corn-stalks and weighted them with hanging pods of young, tender beans. Pictures I saw later of Jack and the Beanstalk always reminded me of this tall corn with bean vines winding around the stalks up to the tassels.

But the one thing my father had brought me to see that de-lighted him most was the pumpkins. I'd never seen so many pumpkins with long necks and small bodies. Pumpkins as big around as the bottom of a flour barrel were sitting in the furrows beneath the tall corn, immovable as rocks. There were pumpkins, and more pumpkins, of all colors—yellow and white, green and brown.

"Look at this, won't you," my father said. "Look what corn, what beans, what pumpkins. Corn ears so big they lean the cornstalks. Beans as thick as honey-locust beans on the honey-locust tree. And pumpkins thicker than the stumps in this new ground. I could walk all over the field on pumpkins and never step on the ground."

He looked upon the beauty of this cove he had cleared and his three crops growing here. He rarely figured a field in dollars and cents. Although he never wasted a dollar, money didn't mean everything to him. He liked to see the beauty of growing things on the land. He carried this beauty in his mind.

Once, when we were walking between cornfields on a rainy Sunday afternoon, he pointed to a redbird on its nest in a locust tree, a redbird with shiny red feathers against the dark back-ground of a nest. It was just another bird's nest to me until he whispered, "Ever see anything as pretty as what the raindrops do to that redbird sitting on her dark nest?" From this day on, I have liked to see birds, especially redbirds, sitting on their nests in the rain. But my father was the first one to make me see the beauty.

He used to talk about the beauty of a rooster redbird, pheasant, chicken hawk, hoot owl, and turkey gobbler. He pointed out the color of the neck, tail, and wing feathers. Then he taught me how to tell a stud terrapin from a female, and a male turtle from a female, a bull blacksnake from a female. My father knew all these things. He learned them in his own way. He observed so closely that he could tell the male from the female in any species, even the gray lizard, which is most difficult.

"A blacksnake is a pretty thing," he once said to me, "so shiny and black in the spring sun after he sheds his winter skin."

He was the first man I ever heard say a snake was pretty. I never forgot his saying it. I can even remember the sumac thicket where he saw the blacksnake.

He saw more beauty in trees than any man I have ever known. He would walk through a strange forest laying his hand upon the trees, saying this oak or that pine, that beech or poplar, was a beautiful tree. Then he would single out other trees and say they should be cut. He would always give his reasons for cutting a tree: too many trees on a root stool, too thick, one damaged by fire at the butt, one leaning against another, too many on the ground, or the soil not deep enough above a ledge of rocks to support them.

Then there were hundreds of times my father took me to the hills to see wild flowers. I thought it was silly at first. He would sit on a dead log, maybe one covered with wild moss, somewhere under the tall beech trees, listening to the wind in the canopy of leaves above, looking at a clump of violets or percoon growing beside a rotted log. He could sit there enjoying himself indefinitely. Only when the sun went down would we get up and start for home.

My father wouldn't break the Sabbath by working, except in an emergency. He would follow a cow that was overdue to calve. He would watch over ewes in the same manner. He followed them to the high cliffs and helped them deliver their lambs, saving their lives. He would do such things on Sundays, and he would fight forest fires. But he always said he could make a living working six days in a week. Yet he was restless on Sundays. He just had to walk around and look over his fields and enjoy them.

Sometimes when I went with my father to a field, we'd cross a stream, and he'd stop the horse, sit down on the bank in the shade, and watch the flow of water. He'd watch minnows in a deep hole. He wouldn't say a word, and I wouldn't either. I'd look all around, wondering what he'd seen to make him stop, but I never would ask him. When he got through looking, he'd tell me why he'd stopped. Sometimes he wouldn't. Then we'd go on to the field together, and he'd work furiously to make up for the time he had lost while he sat beside the stream and watched the clean water flowing over the sand and gravel to some far-off place beyond his little hill world.

My father didn't have to travel over the country searching for something beautiful to see. He didn't have to go away to find beauty, for he found it everywhere around him. He had eyes to find it. He had a mind to know it. He had a heart to appreciate it. He was an uneducated poet of this earth. And if anybody had told him that he was, he wouldn't have understood. He would have turned and walked away without saying anything.

In the winter, when snow was over the ground, and the stars glistened, he'd go to the barn to feed the livestock at four in the morning. I have seen him put corn in the feedboxes for the horses and mules, then go out and stand and look at the morning moon. He once told me he always kept a horse with a flaxen mane and tail because he liked to see one run in the moonlight with his mane arched high and his tail floating on the wind.

I've gone out early in the morning with him, and he's shown me Jack Frost's beautiful architecture, which lasted only until the sun came up. This used to be one of the games my father played with me on a cold morning. He showed me all the designs that I would never have found without him. Today, I cannot look at white fields of frost on early winter mornings and not think of him.

When spring returned, he was always taking me someplace to show me a new tree he had found, or a pretty red mushroom growing on a rotting stump in some deep hollow. He found so many strange and beautiful things that I tried to rival him by making discoveries, too. I looked into the out-of-way and unexpected places to find the beautiful and the unusual.

Once, in autumn, we went to the pasture field to hunt pawpaws. "Look at the golden meat and the big brown seeds like the seeds of a melon or a pumpkin," he said. "Did you ever taste a banana in your life that was as good as a pawpaw? Did you ever see anything prettier than the clean sweet golden fruit of a pawpaw?" I never forgot how he described a pawpaw, and I've always liked their taste.

He took me to the first persimmon grove I ever saw. This was after frost, and the persimmons had ripened and had fallen from the trees. "The persimmon is a candy tree," he said. "It really should have been called the gumdrop tree." I was a small boy then, but ever since I've seen ripe persimmons after frost as brown gumdrops.

I didn't get the idea of dead leaves being golden ships on the sea from a storybook. And neither did my father, for he had never read a book in his life. He'd never had a book read to him either. It was in October, and we were sitting on the bank of W-Branch. We were watching the blue autumn water slide swiftly over the slate rocks. My father picked up leaves that were shaped like little ships and dropped them into the water.

"These are ships on swift water," he told me, "going to far-off lands where strangers will see them." He had a special love for autumn leaves, and he'd pick them up when we were out walking and ask me to identify them. He'd talk about how pretty each leaf was and how a leaf was prettier after it was dead than when it was alive and growing.

Many people thought my father was just a one-horse farmer who never got much out of life. They saw only a little man, dressed in clean, patched overalls, with callused and brier-scratched hands. They often saw the beard along his face. And they saw him go off and just stand in a field and look at something. They thought he was moody. Well, he was that all right, but when he was standing there and people thought he was looking into space, he was looking at a flower or a mushroom or a new bug he'd discovered for the first time. And when he looked up into a tree, he wasn't searching for a hornet's nest to burn or a bird's nest to rob. He wasn't trying to find a bee tree. He was just looking closely at the beauty in a tree. And among the millions, he always found one different enough to excite him.

No one who really knew him ever felt sorry for my father. Any feeling of pity turned into envy. For my father had a world of his own, larger and richer than the vast earth that world travelers know. He found more beauty in his acres and square miles than poets who have written a half-dozen books. Only my father couldn't write down the words to express his thoughts. He had no common symbols by which to share his wealth. He was a poet who lived his life upon this earth and never left a line of poetry— except to those of us who lived with him.

When I was three years old Pa carried me three miles to show me a schoolhouse. He carried me on his back with my arms around his neck; he told me that he was the horse and I was the rider. Pa was a small horse for me to ride. The sweat on his neck wet my arms; the sweat that ran down his body wet his clothes and my legs.

The building was painted white. Pa lifted me from his back to the ground—the first schoolground that I ever put my feet on. Pa pulled a bandanna from his overalls pocket and wiped the sweat from his face and neck.

"I got this house for you, son," he said. "Since I didn't get any education I don't want my youngins to grow up in this world without it. They'll never know what they're missin' until they don't have it. If I could only read and write!"

Though Pa couldn't read and write he served for twenty years as school trustee for the Plum Grove district. I don't believe that a man with a good education could have done better. Pa left his corn in the weeds to go over the district getting the people to petition for the new schoolhouse. He cleared off the schoolground and built the toilets. He built a cistern. There wasn't anything within his power that he wouldn't do for the Plum Grove school.

Pa talked to me about getting an education from the time I can remember. Winter evenings he'd talk to me about going to school to learn to read and write. When I'd ride behind him on the mule, with my arms around his waist, he'd talk about how hard life would be for me if I didn't know how to read and write.

Once, when he was plowing around a steep mountainside, where only a sure-footed mule and a wiry mountain man could stand, Pa rested his mule under a beech. While he rested he made me a small wooden plow with his pocket knife out of a pawpaw sprout. When Pa started his mule around the mountain slope I tried to follow him and make a furrow with my small plow. But I couldn't keep up with him and when he returned on the next furrow he stopped.

"The rows are too long," I said.

"These rows are short," he answered, laughing.

But the rows around this mountainside were long to me; they were long rows for the mule, too. But Pa was in his twenties and tough as hickory bark.

That evening at sundown he walked beside the tired mule and talked to me about going to school soon as the corn was laid by. "There's not a surer way on earth to make a livin' than between the handles of a plow," Pa said. "But I want you to learn to read, write, and cipher some, more than anything else in this world."

At the age of five, I started to the new schoolhouse at Plum Grove. Every afternoon when I came home Pa would ask me how I was getting along. I'd tell him I was getting along all right. We didn't get any report cards in those days. Pa was pleased that I liked to go to school so well. When we 'possum hunted at night with our hounds, all the time he talked to me about school. I was so filled with the idea, I could hardly wait to get to school in the morning and I hated to leave in the afternoon. Saturdays and Sundays my sister and I played school.

"I can do something you can't do," I said to Pa, long before the first school year was over.

"What's that, son?" he asked me.

"I can read and write my name."

My father sat looking at the fire. I didn't know that I had hurt him then; I know now that I did. Not only did I work to be ahead of my sister, Sophia, in school. I worked to get ahead of everybody in my class. And I read every book I could get hold of. Before I was ten years old I was in the seventh grade. I made two grades each year. The teacher told Pa that his children were smart in school, but Pa didn't know how to measure education. He didn't know what it meant to have a ten-year-old pupil in the seventh grade.

Much as Pa believed in school, he had to take me out and hire me out on a farm for twenty-five cents a day. And while I set strawberry plants, while I dug potatoes or cut corn or helped saw tie-timber and bark cross-ties, I wondered how my classmates were getting along at school. My father and his big horse Fred worked for two dollars a day; my mother worked for twenty-five cents a day. We had to have money since our crops had failed two seasons.

How well I remember the first time I went corn cuttin' with my father.

"Son, I want to show you how to cut corn," Pa said to me one misty morning in late September. "You're big enough now to handle a corn-cuttin' knife without hurtin' yourself."

I was nine years old then, but I was tall and sturdy for my age. I watched my father go into the tool shed. When he came out he was carrying a big corn knife in one hand and a small corn knife in the other.

"This knife will be about the right size for you," he said.

Dawn was just breaking as I followed my father's tracks up a little woodland path.

"I'll tell you, son," Pa told me as we waded the carpet of leaves under the trees, "there's nothin' in this world any nicer than a-goin' to the field to cut corn on an early September mornin'. Look at this! It's my favorite time o' year. I want to teach you to look at it this way, son. I want you to know the beauty in it."

Then we came to an opening on the other side of the woods. We had reached the field of corn. It was the side of a mountain. It looked too steep for a shock of corn to stand, but it was typical of the steep mountain slopes in our section. I stood beside my father on the ridgetop and we looked down the mountain at the vast field of corn. Thirty acres spread over a mountainside is a big field of corn.

"Here is where I'll teach you to cut corn," Pa said. "It looks like a big undertakin', but it's not. Cuttin' corn is fast work if you know how. We'll go down and cut up the mountain!"

When we reached the bottom, my father stood a minute and looked up the mountain.

"That's a big field of corn," I said. "It'll take us a long time."

"Not more than a week," Pa laughed. "There's not a job on the farm I'd rather do. It's the prettiest work in the world! Look at this field! Hear the corn blades talkin' to each other? Wonder if they're whisperin' about us comin' across the field with corn knives in our hands! And look," Pa pointed with his knife, "at the colors in the woods."

"This won't be work, son," Pa said as he put a big blue bandanna around his neck. He covered his neck to his chin and tied the bandanna.

"Do like this," he said. "When the sun creeps over the mountain and dries the corn blades they'll scratch your neck. But if you tie your bandanna high on your neck they won't. They'll just rake your face a little, but it won't hurt!"

Then I pulled the big bandanna from my pocket and I wrapped it around my neck just like my father had done.

"We're ready, son," he said. "You watch me. I want you to learn everything about cuttin' corn. First we'll do some countin'."

He counted six rows up the hill from the bottom row.

"We want to cut this corn twelve hills square," he said. "That makes a good average-sized shock of corn. It's big enough to stand against the wind. It's not too big for the fodder to cure well."

Then Pa counted six corn hills from the end of the field on the sixth row. And here he reached into the seventh row and bent over two stalks of corn and began wrapping their tops around the tops of the hills directly below until he had made them the shape of an oxbow. He wrapped them until he had made a substantial thing that looked like a tall spider with four strong legs. "This is what you call a rider," he said. "It's the underpinnin' of the corn shock. It must be made strong so it'll hold the corn shocks against the strong winds."

In the sixth row from where we had tied the first rider, he counted twelve hills of corn, and then I watched him bend two corn hills from the seventh row down to two corn hills in the sixth row and wrap the stalks until he had made another rider.

"It's always best to go through the field and tie a row of riders," he said. "Then come back through the field and cut corn and put around them. I'll show you how."

Before Pa had finished tying the row of riders through the field, he let me try to tie one. And while I worked, he laughed.

"It's not a bad rider. You're a-learnin' fast. Now we'll start cuttin'," he said. He showed me how to swing the knife away from myself. Then he showed me how to let the cornstalks balance across my arm as I cut.

"This is tall corn for you to handle, son," he said. "But you can do it. Now you cut the seventh and eighth rows so you can carry downhill. I'll cut the sixth and fifth rows and carry them uphill. And I'll tie the middle-bands."

"What are the middle-bands?" I asked.

"When we put four rows into the shock we tie a band around

it," he laughed. "This will strengthen the shock. Not many corn cutters do this. And their corn shocks tumble over when they get wet or we have a wind storm. You know, I seldom ever have a shock fall. This is the secret why so many people want me to cut corn for 'em."

Cutting corn was awkward to me. But I liked it, because I could see behind me white knees of the cornstalks where my knife had gone through them. And when I took away the tall corn and left a spot of barren ground this gave me the feeling I was doing something. And my father, known as the finest corn cutter for miles around, was teaching me how.

And soon we had cut four rows through the field, and had tied the middle-bands. It was a clean swath through the tall corn except for the corn knees, and they stood with their white tops in long pretty rows.

"I love this work," I told Pa. "I like everything that goes on around me in the autumn weather."

"I told you cuttin' corn was like play," Pa smiled happily now that he had encouraged me to see what he had always seen while he cut corn. "We'll finish cuttin' our corn, then we'll cut corn for other people."

Then Pa showed me how he could really cut corn. He had been fooling around to show me how. He started at the far end of the field with his four rows. He cut them and carried loads up the hill and placed them securely around the middle-bands. And I tried to follow him. But I couldn't.

I did cut faster, though, while the leaves, like birds, blew over me on the morning wind gusts. And the insects sang their cheery songs to me. The corn blades whispered to me. I had the feeling of accomplishment even if I couldn't cut corn half as fast as my father. He cut his four rows to the far end of the field and then he came back and met me on my rows.

"This is the way to cut corn," Pa said. "This is railroadin' corn!"

Then I bent the stalks while my father tied two bands around each shock. And when we had tied the long row of cornstalks, I looked at our accomplishment with delight.

"They look like wigwams," I said. "Look at 'em! Look what a pretty row of wigwams! Thirty wigwams!"

My father laughed. Then he looked at his watch.

"Time to go to dinner," he said. "This is not a bad mornin's work. I have cut fifty by myself in a half-day. But I've never been able to cut a hundred shocks in a day."

I followed my father through the cornfield toward the ridge-top. Then I followed him through the woods where the golden, rust-colored, silver, brown, and scarlet drops of leaf-rain slithered from the tall treetops through the bright autumn wind to the ground.

"Are we goin' to cut corn this afternoon?" I asked.

"Why not?" he said.

"Hardly anybody around here cuts corn in the afternoon," I said. "Uncle Mel never does. He says the dry corn blades scratch his neck and face."

Pa laughed the loudest he had laughed all day.

"That's why your Uncle Mel always has to hire me to help him," he said. "Sure, we're goin' to work this afternoon. It's just as much fun to cut corn in the afternoon as it is in the mornin'."

That afternoon Pa and I cut another row of corn shocks around the mountain slope. The dry corn blades did rake our faces above the bandannas. But we didn't mind. We "railroaded" the corn. The corn blades talked to one another more than they did when they were damp with morning mists. And the songs of the insects were cheerier. The leaves blew over us, and the autumn wind, laden with lush mellow fragrance of ripening grain, wild grapes, and nuts dried the sweat on our hot faces.

That week I worked with my father doing something I loved to do. He had taught me from the age of six when I went to the fields with him that work with my hands was honorable. I had never liked some of the things I had done, such as the back-breaking jobs of thinning corn and setting tobacco. But I had never enjoyed play any more than I enjoyed cutting corn.

And from day to day, as the week passed on, I never grew tired of it. I went to bed hoping the night would soon pass so I could get back to the big cornfield. Saturday afternoon, late, after one week's work, we had finished cutting our field of corn. We counted four hundred fifty-five corn shocks, standing straight and pretty and tied tightly and neatly at the tops. This is a great Indian Village, I thought, as I looked the field over with pride.

"Next week we'll cut Mel's corn," Pa said. "Soon as we have finished with his, we'll cut Bill Duncan's. Others have asked me to cut their corn. We'll get two thousand shocks to cut before the

season's over. But we can do it, son! We can do it together! You're
a real corn cutter!"

Just think, I'll get to help cut two thousand shocks of corn, I
thought, as I followed in Pa's footsteps down the path where a
shower of September leaves rained gently upon us.

Beyond Dark Hills

WHEN SCROLL PRESS of Howe, Oklahoma, published Stuart's small collection of poems titled *Harvest of Youth* in 1930, the young writer immediately suppressed it because the fact that Scroll was a vanity press embarrassed him. On the other hand, when *Man with a Bull-Tongue Plow* was published in 1934, Stuart launched himself as a poet worthy of the attention of such literary figures as Malcolm Cowley. Before the publication of *Man with a Bull-Tongue Plow*, however, came the writing of *Beyond Dark Hills*, the first of six autobiographical books treating education as a major theme. Stuart describes the writing of the book and the circumstances out of which he wrote it in the book itself. Although written in eleven days in March and April of 1932, *Beyond Dark Hills* was revised and expanded before it was finally published in 1938 by Dutton. Because of the book's popularity, McGraw-Hill published a new edition in 1972. Reviews indicate that both editions were well received.

As for the 1938 publication by Dutton, in "Jesse Stuart's Autobiography Reveals Poet," a review for the *St. Paul Dispatch* (20 April 1938), James Gray commented on the poetic quality of the work, a comment quite common among reviewers. Marion Leland likened the writer of *Beyond Dark Hills* to a meandering stream in his presentation and the story to a free-flowing mountain stream (*Greenwich [Connecticut] Press*, 28 April 1938), and H.R. Pinckard called the book unsophisticated but "desperately earnest" (*Huntington Herald Advertiser*, 24 April 1938). Carl Van Doren titled his review "In *Beyond Dark Hills* Jesse Stuart Begins His Autobiography" (*Boston Herald*, 23 April 1938), and William E. Wilson saw the book as presenting a complete picture of Stuart in its crudity as well as its beauty (*Providence Journal*, 24 April 1938). On the other hand, when the McGraw-Hill edition was published in 1972, the reviewers in general agreed with Barbara Hunter in lauding it as "more of a treasure" than when it was written in 1932 (*Vallejo Times-Herald,* 3 December 1972). Ralph Hollenbeck wrote that the new edition provided a glimpse into a past that had persisted into the present (*Seattle Post-Intelligencer,* 10 September 1972), and Ethel Jacobson saw it as addressing the generation gap between the student-author and the man looking back (*St. Louis Post-Dispatch,* 27 August 1972). Finally, Charlotte S. Harris noted that Stuart's philosophy of life was inherent in his philosophy of death as expressed in *Beyond Dark Hills* (*Jackson [Tennessee] Sun,* 19 November 1972). In any event, it seems that the decision by McGraw-Hill to publish a new edition in 1972 was more than justified because by then Stuart's readers had a much larger sample of his work against which to evaluate it. Besides *Harvest of Youth* and *Man with a Bull-Tongue Plow,* the only other book Stuart had published before the first edition of *Beyond Dark Hills* was a collection of stories titled *Head o' W-Hollow* (1936).

The composing of *Beyond Dark Hills* took place at Vanderbilt University during the Great Depression, and in the book Stuart contends that he could not write a passing term paper: "When I started to write a term paper I would write a poem." Dr. Edwin Mims asked each student to write an autobiographical paper of about eighteen pages, and Stuart set out to please his teacher. When he finished, he had 322 closely written pages. Dr. Mims read Stuart's paper closely, after which he commented: "I have been teaching school for forty years and I have never read anything so crudely written and yet beautiful, tremendous, and powerful as that term paper you have written." Various scholars, including Lee Oly Ramey, have checked details with Professor Mims concerning the term paper only to be referred to the story as Stuart told it: "There is not much more to say than Stuart says in his *Beyond Dark Hills.* He tells the story rather accurately. That was, of course, the most remarkable term paper I ever got from a student" (Letter to Ramey, 2 December 1939).

Continuing the chronology begun in the first selection, "Early Education," the selection included here is not the colorful story of pain, hunger, and disappointment characterizing the Vanderbilt years. Rather it is of the high school years. Titled "Opossums and Poetry" and constituting the third chapter of *Beyond Dark Hills,* it is a story of adolescence in which a boy from the hills searches for an identity only to find that he is caught between two ways of life—one belonging to the dark hills and the other beyond them. It is a powerful story of education and conflict ending with Stuart's realization that he would have to leave.

After the first crops were laid by on our own land, there was part of the summer left. I would go and find a job. I needed the money. I went four miles over the bony ridge to the little town of Greenup. The town was in the process of being overhauled. There were electric wires being put upon poles. The alleys were being paved and the main streets of the town. The contractors were crying for help. They wanted farm boys, I heard. Well, this was the place to get work.

I began to work for John Pancake. My work was taking a pick and tearing old stones out of the street. They were buried under the oily dirt that had been smeared in July with oil to hold down the dust. The work paid well, I thought. I made thirty cents an hour. I worked ten hours a day and on Saturday until noon. That was really hard work and the walk back home made my legs stiff at night and my hands hurt. One day we were working under an elm shade. Three husky farm boys "white-eyed" on the job and asked the boss for their money. An old man seventy years old working beside me said: "Look at that, won't you. Them big strong devils won't work when they can get it. That's what's a-matter with our country today—jist sicha fellars as them. They need their blocks knocked off. Then they'd have a little sense maybe."

It was on the following day some extravagant man bought a green watermelon. A boy standing on the street said to me: "Hit me on the nose, I dare you." He put his finger on his nose. I hadn't finished the melon but I let the piece I was eating cover his whole face. "You are fired!" shouted the boss. He was standing behind a tree. Then the old man that had talked about the men that "white-eyed" the day before said: "What is this world a-coming to, anyway? They didn't act that a-way when I was a shaver a-kicking up my heels." In two hours I was working for the concrete gang. They didn't know I had been fired from the other gang. I told that boss the other fellow had sent me there—said he was working too many men as it was. "W'y hell! I can't work any more men. Oh, let me see. I can use you over there dumping sacks of concrete into the mixer. How is your flesh? Can it stand concrete against it in July? You know that damn cement is hard on the skin when you sweat. It takes off the hide." "I can stand it if the other men have stood it," I told him. I got the job.

September came and the wires had been tied to the tall poles. "Them are live wires," said an old man; "touch one and your soul will be blasted into eternity. Funny how smart people are getting to be. This world can't last much longer." The main street was a white walk of smooth concrete and the yellow elm leaves were skipping along on it. The concrete mixer was moved around in front of a schoolhouse. When I saw that schoolhouse I had many thoughts. I would go home and get my sister and we would come to this place to school. It was a beautiful place, a bluish-gray brick building with a spire shooting above the tops of the elm trees. I saw the children going there and they were all well dressed. I wanted to go there. I told the boss to pay me off.

The next Monday morning Sis and I walked under the tall door when the bell sounded. I remember hearing a red-headed girl say, "I get mixed up when I talk to the teacher about the bell. You know, when I sleep late of a morning and have to talk to her about it. I don't know how to say that *ring, rang* and *rung*. I get them all mixed up. Oh, what is the use of all this schooling anyway? I'll clerk in the old man's store some day anyway!" I thought that was funny. She was afraid of three words. I would just say one. What did it matter, right or wrong? I wouldn't be afraid, at least.

The students did not take to us very well. I remember a boy saying, "That Stuart girl is right good-looking if she had good clothes to wear." One day a skinny boy asked me what I knew about the price of eggs. I asked him what he knew about the length of mattock handles. The students standing near all laughed. That was a great place, I thought. I saw many boys wearing fine clothes I envied. I wanted a long red sweater like Burl Mavis wore and a necktie like the one I had seen Fred Mansfield wear. I wanted many things I could not get. When I ate my lunch that I brought wrapped in a newspaper, I always got away from the other boys. I went around by the old flour mills. I didn't want them to see biscuits with meat and mustard between, and the cornbread.

School work was not hard for me. And I would hear the boys by the houses along the streets tell their mothers that the work was terribly hard at school. Some spoke of the teachers being unfair. That was funny too. We walked eight miles each day and helped to do the work at home. When we had an algebra test Burl Mavis sat beside me and called me Stuart. At other times he told me to get the hayseed out of my hair. The greatest enjoyment I could have was to work a problem when the rest of the class had failed. I did this a few times. One day Miss Hamilton said: "There is a Patrick Henry in this room. Now you just wait and see. To whom do you think I refer?"

"Oh, you are referring to me," shouted many of the boys.

"No," said she, "there he is."

She pointed to me. After that the students would pass me and giggle: "Patrick Henry, how about 'Give me liberty or give me death'?" they would say. That year I made three B pluses and one A. My sister made four A's. But that place was great, I thought, and I'd like to be a teacher in a big school like that. A teacher there was something.

I asked one of the old men about how old the schoolhouse was. I had noticed that the steps were wearing thin. "I don't know," said one. "My Grandpa Jake Filson went around there. It is mighty old, son. I just can't tell you. But I know things have changed mightily since I was a boy and went there." I learned later that it was one of the oldest schools on the Ohio River. Then I asked Miss Lykins one day the oldest college in America. She said it was Harvard. I told her I wanted to go there to college some day. She looked at me in a funny way. Then I asked her more questions. She was very kind.

My father would say now: "Yes, go on to school and get an education. I want you to do something with your head as well as your hands. I don't want you to have to work like I have. Go on to school." And my mother would say, "My oldest children are in high school," when she wrote a letter to one of her brothers or to her sister.

The bell rang the hour school closed. Miss Lykins met us in her office and gave us our report cards. She said: "The school year is over now. I hope you have enjoyed it. Here are your report cards."

That summer I went back to the farm. It was not the same place. I wanted to think about the town over the bony ridge—Greenup. I could see that white concrete and the yellow leaves drifting over it. I could see the happy, well-dressed girls going along talking about nothing in particular. There was that flashy red sweater Burl Mavis wore. I could see Fred Mansfield's pretty necktie. Lord, there was lots to live for and the world was big.

I plowed in the oats early that spring before school was out. They were green on the hillsides now. The young rabbits played among them. The cows that had been used to woodland pasture stepped out on timothy and orchard grasses this summer. The martins came back to their boxes. The honeybees played over the wild plum trees that grew in a cove at the back of the house. But these things were not the same. When I turned the furrows on the hillsides I did not think of the tall corn that would soon be growing there—nor did I dream of the snow on the ground and the big white ears of corn in the crib with a split-bottom feed basket at the front door. I didn't care much about the crows and the cow birds that followed the furrow after me. "Them cow birds are funny things," said Uncle Rank Larks. "They lay their eggs in other birds' nests. The other birds hatch out their young and raise them. They are durn funny things."

My father worked away now. I was the boss on the farm. I planted the corn. I planted the potatoes. I sowed the cane hay. I prepared the land for tobacco. It was a big job for me. My mother, my sister Mary, and James worked in the fields with me. I did the plowing and I selected the grounds for certain grains. And since I was boss my orders were to clean the corn and tobacco well the first time—get every weed. "Don't leave a weed in any row. Clean the stumps well. I like to see the fields clean. The corn isn't smothered then."

"There is a hurricane of weeds in that piece up in the hollow. We must get to it soon, son," my mother would say. My father would say: "That boy of mine is tearing that place all to pieces. I'd put him against any man in the country. He's worked them mules down lean." Uncle Rank Larks would say, "Mitch Stuart, with a family to work like yourn you ought to be independent rich." When I sat down at the table at home it was: "Now children, eat something that will stick to the ribs. Don't mince around over the sweet stuff too much. You'll be hungry before night comes."

I wanted to get the corn laid by as soon as possible this summer. I had heard of a military camp where boys got their way paid there and back and all expenses while they were there. I put in my application. I was fifteen and the first boy in the county to try it.

That summer was a hot one. But we had plenty of rain and plenty of weeds. The corn shot up out of the earth. It was a fine season. The beans covered the corn and the pumpkins lay over the fields. It was all over and the season was a glorious one. Mom would pickle her beans now, can the peaches and berries and later make apple butter and wild grape jelly. There are so many things for a woman to do on a farm about this time of year. And my mother was called over the country for sickness. She would get out of bed at midnight and go. It did not matter, rain or shine, when a child was sick she would go. But above all the time it took to do this work she found time to work on her quilts. She would go out and find a wild flower she liked. Then she would make the same kind of flower with quilt pieces. She loved to do it. She would sit far into the night looking at the beauty in a new design she was creating.

After the season was done with, I took the mules to the pasture and gave them their freedom. Their manes and tails could grow out now and their hoofs grow long. I did not care. I was ready to leave for a place below Louisville, Kentucky. I wanted the trip. I had never been fifty miles away from home before, and this was three hundred. And I collected the mattocks, spades and plows and hoes and put them in the shed. The season was over.

The trip to Camp Knox was the trip of my life. I took the longest way possible on Government money. I went to North Vernon, Indiana, then I turned directly south to Louisville. At Camp Knox I found that a fifteen-year-old farm boy, six feet tall and weighing one hundred and ten pounds, was too much out of place. "Did you bring a bottle along, Gawky?" said a gentleman from a north Ohio town. "I don't know whether you would call it a bottle or not," I said. "We'll see." I pulled a blank pistol from my pocket which I had brought for curiosity. He made his way rapidly through the crowd. When the other boys saw the gun was a fake they laughed. But Camp Knox was a torture to me. I was put in the awkward squad for throwing my rifle to a Captain when he asked for one. I was kept there three days for that offense. I was given a cold mud bath for throwing a bucket of water on the corporal in charge of the barracks. I was placed on K.P. for coming to reveille with my shoes unlaced and leggings left in the barracks. I did not conform very well to military rules and regulations. Then the fellows tossed me up and let me fall back on a blanket. I went through the blanket to the ground. I was sore for weeks. They only laughed about it. That was why I threw the water on the corporal. He had a hand in it. I actually cried when I was put on the awkward squad for speaking at attention. But it did no good. The army is no place for tears. But I excelled in doing exercises and shooting. I loved to do them. I learned them all and the counts they were done in.

When I reached home again I was glad to see the hills. I went out and looked over the corn. And I said: "My, how this corn has grown! It is as big as it will ever be. The cane hay is ready to cut. The potatoes are ready to dig. And it will soon be time to start off to school again." I was glad to get back home and hold my brother and sisters spellbound about Camp Knox and Louisville. I had only been in Louisville twice and that was passing through both times. But I had big tales to tell about everything but K.P. and the awkward squad. I never mentioned them.

Autumn came again. The oak trees in northeast Kentucky were shedding their leaves. The flying leaves were of many colors. The crows began to go in pilfering trains over the country. And wild geese went southward with many a honking cry. It was all beautiful back there and the best place in the world after all. The corn was getting ready to cut now. The brown fields of heavy corn looked very pleasant. It was the victory of hard labor.

My sophomore year in Greenup High School was a happy time in my life. When I went back to Greenup I felt just about the equal of Burl Mavis. "I would be better than Burl," I let myself think, "if I only had some clothes." I had an idea—two of them. I could buy my own books, my sister's books and buy myself some clothes. I would ask my father's permission to make crossties from the timber on the farm to sell. I would hunt the fur-bearing animals in those surrounding hills with old Black-Boy. I could make money. I was too tall now to wear knee pants. And I was getting too old to wear them now.

I started making crossties in our barn lot. I could make them well, I found out. I would cut down a black oak tree. Then I would measure eight and a half feet. I would hack that place with the ax, trim the branches from the tree and measure another length and so on. Then, I would measure the thickness of the crosstie on the body of the tree—hack little lines to score by. Then I would smooth down the sides with a broad ax. My brother would help me to saw the ties apart. I would bark them and they would be ready for market. On a bet one day I made twenty-two crossties and got them ready for the wagon. Many people doubt that but it is an actual fact. If you know anything about timber, you'll know that is a day's work. I made my father's timber up so rapidly that he stopped me. But I had fifty dollars now. I went to Ironton, Ohio, and bought myself a long suit of clothes. It was a gray tweed suit and cost me eighteen dollars. I bought shirts, ties and socks. I gave my sister some money and bought our books.

There came a frost and hit the corn. The blades turned white and began to fall. "Save that feed, son. The cattle will need it this winter. You will have to miss school long enough to cut that knob piece of corn." "I'll cut it all on Saturday," I said. That Saturday I dressed well to keep the blades from cutting my face and hands. I "railroaded" the corn from daylight until four o'clock that afternoon. I cut it twelve hills square on a steep hillside. I tied one middle band around the shocks and two outward bands to make it stand well. My father would not believe that I had cut fifty-four shocks until he counted them. He opened his eyes wider when I went back that night and cut twenty-four by moonlight. "Go to the store and get anything you want. My credit is good and nothing I've got is too good for a boy that will work like you." The corn was out of danger now. The frost-bitten blades were safe for the cattle. "It is a great thing to have a strong body," I have often thought.

I would take Black-Boy and go into the woods at night. I would go alone for miles and miles. I would trust Black-Boy quicker than I would any person I knew. Black-Boy was a powerful cur. He had hound blood in him. "A little hound blood gives a dog a good nose." He had strong front legs, a heavy pair of shoulders, a thin body near his hips. He was built for speed, power and endurance. He was as vicious as he was powerful. I was not afraid to go anywhere with Black-Boy. I knew the kind of affection he had for me in a time of danger. Though he was nine years old now and his face was getting gray his teeth were still good. On a night's hunt I would take a lantern, a coffee sack, a mattock and a couple of books. I would go off in a silent dark hollow and tie the lantern to a tree. I would sit at the base of the tree and study plane geometry and read English—especially the poetry of Robert Burns. I would get interested and Black-Boy would tree. If he barked fast I knew I must hurry. If he barked slowly I took my time. When I got to him sometimes he would be fighting an opossum. I would put it in the coffee sack and move on to another patch of woods. He would run and bark in an old field. I knew what that was. It was a skunk. I hated to handle them but there was the money. A skunk hide would bring from one to seven dollars.

This would go on some nights all night long. I have caught as many as eleven opossums with Black-Boy in one night. That was on a night when he didn't find a skunk. The scent of a skunk always hurt his nose. He could not smell as well afterwards. For miles and miles around my home I knew where every persimmon tree of any importance was. I knew where the pawpaw patches were. I went to those places for opossums. I got them there. Black-Boy went just as strong at three o'clock in the morning as he did when we started, if he didn't run across a skunk. And one night I remember getting four skunks and one opossum. I made money that night. I hunted over those hills night after night during the autumn season.

There was loneliness in the dark hills when the wind stirred the withered leaves on the trees. It was music to me. It was poetry. It hangs to me better than a piece of clothing for it fits me well and will not wear out. Black-Boy's bark grew to be beautiful to my ear. It was the assurance of something in the darkness of a night. A dog's voice that you know out in a lonely place does you good to hear. Persimmon tree leaves and the yellow leaves on a poplar tree are beautiful at night when a dull moon is shining barely over the hill top. A gray opossum in a persimmon tree is something you like to shake to the ground with a shower of small reddish leaves falling like a little shower of rain. And then when the rain fell it was the time to hunt. The forest is so silent. Opossums love quiet woods. They are afraid of wind in the brush or the rattle of dead leaves. And when the rain thug-thugs—slowly at night— the skunks come out to root their noses into the dirt in the old fields. But skunk scent at night will knock one down if it is raining, it is so strong.

Many boys asked me to let them hunt with me. I would not

take them. They wanted to bring guns and shoot. They wanted to build fires in the woods and go away and leave them. I thought they didn't know how to hunt. I knew old Black-Boy wouldn't hunt with a bunch like that. He was too old at the trade. He would go back to the house. I would not hunt with any of them.

I sold the opossums. I sold them to the Negroes and I got the hides back. One shipment of fur I recall getting forty-three dollars for. Then there was the fun of hunting. The boys would say to me: "Where do you find all them opossums? We can't find them." "For two reasons," I would answer. "First, you don't know how to hunt. Second, your dog isn't any good. His nose is not made right. He has no hound blood in him." On windy nights man must seek the low quiet valleys for opossums. On still damp nights, the hilltops and the old fields. Again you must keep your mouth shut and never crowd a dog. Go quietly like an Indian. Always keep in mind the pawpaw trees and the persimmon trees.

I would take Black-Boy when game began to get scarce in the black oak hills and go into the old fields near the town of Green-up. There I found plenty of game. I sat down to figure it out. Fur-bearing creatures are not fools. They learn the fields that are molested less by man and dogs. After I had hunted a valley out, I would tell the boys where I had been getting the game. They were always silly enough to follow where I had gone.

This was the year that I began to try writing poetry. It was because of the wind I heard in the dead leaves and the loneliness of sounds at night, not to mention the influence Robert Burns had on me. This was my first year to study literature. I had the course under a Southern woman, Mrs. Robert Hatton. She read poetry well. She stressed Robert Burns because she loved his verse. I would read his poetry every spare minute I had. I carried his poems wherever I went. I thought I had never heard words more beautiful than those in "Flow Gently, Sweet Afton." It was sung in school once or twice each week. The sentiment of that song choked me, for I loved it deeply. And there was "Highland Mary," "John Anderson My Jo," and "The Cotter's Saturday Night." I feasted on the poetry of Robert Burns. It seemed as if something big in life had taken hold of me. I wanted to write poetry like Robert Burns. He was a Scottish plowboy. I read all that in his life. I knew it didn't always take the boys that wore sweaters like Burl Mavis to do things. And my prayer, if I ever prayed one then, was to write poetry that would endure like the poetry of Robert Burns.

I would go home at night and tell my mother that I wanted to do something in life. I told her my plans at the milk gap every evening after spring came on and the cows were turned out on the grass. The second year of high school had taken hold of me tremendously. My mother would be surprised at the things I said to her. She would say: "You know, sometimes I have felt like I would just like to get out and go and go and go. I have felt that these hills could not hold me. And if I had been a man I would have gone. But now, you see, I am a mother tied down with a family and I cannot go. I want to stay and take care of my children. They are all I have that I care anything about. I want to see them well-raised to be young men and women. And when they go out into the world, I want people to say there is a respectable family of children—the children of Martha Stuart. She tried her best to raise them right and she did."

We would talk on at the milk gap. I would try to milk a cow. She would kick the bucket out of my hand. I would want to hit the cow with a stick. "You mustn't hit one of the cows. They feed you half you eat. The way you like milk and then hit a cow! Here, put my apron on and you can milk that cow. My cows are not used to men folks." I put the apron on. The cow stands perfectly still. Now I set the bucket on the ground and zig-zag two streams of white milk into the zinc two-gallon water bucket. "You are ruining these cows feeding them middlings and cow feed when the timothy is knee-high." "They are always right at this gap morning and night for the handful of middlings I feed them. I do not have to go through the wet weeds to hunt them. No one is here to get them since you go to school in the springtime now and your father works away. It is so lonesome to hunt the cows and hear the whippoorwills a-callin'."

It is lonesome to hear the whippoorwills calling and walk over the new-plowed fields in April. When I came in from school I would pull off my shoes and slip into the silence of the evening woods. I would steal quietly. I would watch the young rabbits play in the pasture. I would hear the crows caw-caw in the pine trees. I would take a paper and pencil and go to the pine grove over from the house and write my themes. The teacher would say: "There is a flavor of the soil and a picture of the sky and the trees in your themes."

The time was here to sow lettuce and tobacco beds. It was the time to take the mules and go into the fields and plow all day long. James was big enough now to keep the stalks and sprouts cut ahead of the plow. But he was only six and when night came he would be very tired. We took our lunch to the field in a gallon lard bucket and tied it up to a locust limb with a string, to keep the ants out of it. We brought two bottles of milk and put them in a deep blue hole of creek water to keep it cool. When night came the sweaty mules were glad when they heard me say "Whoa-ho, Jack and Barnie, whoa-ho." They stopped breathlessly still. Then I would unhook the rusty trace chains and wrap them around a rump piece of the harness to keep them from dragging on the mules' heels. James would ride one mule and lead the other. I would carry the dinner bucket and milk bottles and a load of stove wood back to the house. "It don't look right and it ain't right for a man to work a brute all day and ride it home at night," my father used to say when we worked in the fields together.

When the red worms came to the top of the ground around the hog pen it was time to go fishing. We would dig red-worm bait and then go to the branch and seine minnows with a coffee sack for bait. "Them craw-dads ain't very good bait. I can't have any luck with them," Uncle Rank Larks would always say. James and I would go to the W-Hollow creek. I would teach him how to fish before we went to Little Sandy. I would take a minnow hook. I would catch a fly with my hand—put it on the hook and drop it with a little thug into the water. The minnows would fight over it before one could swallow it. Finally the bottle cork would go under the water and I'd flip the string tied to the end of the short pole. A silver-colored minnow would gape and wiggle in the wind. "Stand back here so a minnow can't see you. It is always better. Go silently and never shake the brush along the bank. It will be better, you'll learn later. But this doesn't have anything to do with fishing in Little Sandy—only you must learn to keep quiet when you fish and wait a long, long time for a bite sometimes. But keep at it. Change your bait when they don't bite. Different kinds of fish have different tastes. Try many foods on them. And whatever you do don't drink water out of these streams. They are dangerous to human flesh." James learned to catch minnows first. He later learned to fish.

But against what I warned him about the treacherous streams, one hot June day he drank from a stream. Typhoid fever was the result and it lasted for five weeks. One leg was left lame. "The water was clear as the sky," he said, "and it looked good to drink. It was pretty water and it tasted good." Do not be deceived by the crystal clearness of high hill water. It is full of thousands of germs that will put you flat on your back in less than seven days after you drink them. You will want to die. But you can't die sometimes and sometimes you do die against your will. But your bones ache and your flesh is hot. I have been that way twice because I drank of that beautiful liquid—cool to the parched lips and fine to the taste, yet treacherous as a copperhead.

Once I drank of blue mountain water under the shade of beech trees. I went above and found a dead horse in the stream and two spotted hound dogs pulling carrion from his flanks. I wanted to vomit but I could not. The buzzards sat upon a dead oak limb in the sun and waited for their share. The buzzards are worth thousands of dollars and save many lives by cleaning the carrion off the land. I know of nothing but a copperhead's head that they won't eat. A copperhead's head is the most poisonous of flesh. A hog will eat all of a copperhead but its head. This is the way of mountain streams. When beasts of the land and the birds of the air know they are sick enough to die they go for water. Water has a great healing power for a feverish body. When they come to the stream they gorge on water and die by the stream. If a skunk gets his leg cut off between the steel jaws of a trap he will die by a stream of running water if he is to die at all. The same is true of the fox and the rabbit.

This was the time of year I would go to the old orchards near home. I would see the apple trees white with blossom. The wind would blow through their tops and blow the blossoms to the ground. I would think of the thought I had about man and the seasons. These apple trees were only treacherous. They would bloom again next April. But I would never be as young again as I was that day. My season only came once. I would bloom but once and then I would go back to the earth and be silent and cold forever. I would walk under the trees and hear the wind blow. I would see a buzzard fly over the trees in bloom and then I would think of carrion—dead horses by the sky-blue streams. The shoe-makes would be leafing now—those little red sticky leaves with a sour smell on damp days. "It looks like a hound dog with a good nose will get his nostrils filled with the scent," I liked to think.

Later the blackberry briars bloomed beneath the apple trees and the wind off the blackberry blossoms is enough to make man jealous of bees. It is enough to make him want to live forever. It is enough to make him want to write poetry. It is enough to make him want to shout to the wind, the sky and the stars: "I have something to say. Won't you listen to me for a moment? My voice is not strong, but won't you listen? I tell you again and again I have something to say. I have walked in the silence of the night. I have talked to the stars. I have tried to be strong as the oak trees I have leaned against and on whose bark I have put my hands. I have clenched my teeth to keep from crying when the wild geese flew over the brown autumn fields with their honk-honking cries. I wanted to follow them. I have lived among the things I loved. I have put my hands on them. I have talked to them but they could not understand. Now I have something to say to you. I want to say it in words beautiful as the stars. Can't you listen to my voice while I am still beneath these blooming apple trees?"

During the second summer of my high school career, I farmed. And again the corn crops were heavy. We cleaned new land each spring and sowed the old in grass. "It pays a body not to run his land too long in corn in these hills. They are never the same any more." The fruit trees grew faster than the corn—long, healthy-looking slick-bark appletree branches and smooth-bodied cherry trees. The peach trees looked like rank red switches in the wind for the leaves are small and the body of the tree shows well. The crop was all done a second season since I had been boss on the small place. I didn't set out much tobacco. It took all the time between July and September when I wanted to be free to hunt and swim and ride the mules. I would not go back to that army camp at Camp Knox. I didn't want to any more. "You do this. You do that. You are in the army. Bristle up. This evening comes parade. You'd better watch about not saluting an officer. It is the uniform and what it represents that you salute." This summer I took a supply of Tennyson's poetry and the songs of Robert Burns and went to live at Carter Caves. I went with Tillman Cartwell.

We took a small tent and lived in a place called Horseshoe Bottom. That was a drowsy place there.

We would fish all day long. We made a raft to sit on and fish. But the turtles were vicious and would take our bait. We could not swim in the clear waters of Tygart for turtles. I would sit upon the banks and knock them off logs and rocks down in the river with a twenty-two. "Where did you learn to shoot that way, Stuart—Camp Knox last summer?" "Hell, no. Not in any army. They don't teach you to shoot. I got it shooting squirrels out of the tall walnut trees near home. Hunting for myself. I take pride in my shooting and hunting. Watch me knock that little turtle down on the rock." Tillman would let me use the rifle after he saw me shoot. I killed bullfrogs, squirrels and several ground hogs. We ate the squirrels and bullfrogs but Tillman wouldn't touch a piece of ground hog and they were fat on the earing corn. They make a great dish but Tillman couldn't cook them. I tried to show him how Mom rolled them in meal and baked them. But I had forgotten how myself if I had ever really learned. "Them ground hogs are clean things and man won't eat them," said Farmer Rankins, "yet they eat hogs and chickens. There ain't anything dirtier than a chicken."

Often in my walks around the caves I found old bones. I shall never forget the hum of the bees around Carter Caves. They were feeding on buckwheat. My, how they love buckwheat blossoms! The fields were filled with blossoms and the blossoms were filled with bees. The black locust trees were blooming too. The bees were working on them and on the shoe-makes, but not like they were working on the buckwheat.

I would sit at the mouth of a cool cave and read Tennyson for hours. When I left there, I left my books in this cave. I never went back for them. I wrote and told Farmer Rankins he could have them for the many good meals I had eaten with him. I directed him in the letter to the cave. "Upon a shelf of rocks when you first go in at the entrance," I said, "you'll find them, away from the dripping water."

When the last food we had was eaten, we started the twenty-mile walk to the railroad station. We were on our way back to Greenup. Tillman Cartwell would enter school that year as a freshman. He would get along fine.

Tillman's people had graduated from the school. He said to

me: "You must come to visit me, Stuart. I want my mother to know you." "You must come to visit me, Tillman," I said, half hoping that he would never come. My home was not what he was used to and my people were only educated to the soil. Tillman was one of the boys who had once asked me to hunt with him. He asked to go into the woods with me and Black-Boy. I thought he was giddy like some of the fellows there. I always got around taking him. Now I was sorry I hadn't taken him with me before.

Back to school again. The pigskin was flying in the air again. I had always thought I would play when I put on some weight. The big fellows had graduated off the team. I was getting to be one of the big fellows there now. Tillman said, "Get in there, Stuart. You can make the team. You're tough as Spikey. He made it his first year out."

I was introduced to Rawl Briswell. He was the bully of the town and the school's bad boy. It wasn't anything uncommon to see a boy with blood running out of his nose. Ask what was wrong, and a boy would say, "W'y, Rawl Briswell hit him." Rawl was six feet two and weighed nearly two hundred pounds. The boys in school were afraid of Rawl. He knew it too. He would slap them around any way he pleased. If they didn't like it he would slap them again. Nothing was said for there was nothing to say, only that Rawl Briswell did it. There was nothing to do about it. This was his fourth year in school and he would have one more year to finish. He stayed to play football and fight, everybody thought. "John Briswell's boy don't go to that school for any good. He just goes there to bully the boys around and to fight. It's a bad streak running through his blood."

Tillman Cartwell told me one day that he had heard Rawl talking about me coming in from the country and getting cocky. He told Tillman he was going to take some of it, if not all of it, out of me with his fist. He said he thought he would do it before the day was over. Tillman warned me to watch him. I knew that he was foul in a football game. He would spit his opponent's eyes full of tobacco spittle. The next time he would slug him under the chin with his fist. I have seen boys carried from the field when Rawl hit them. The referee was not wise enough to catch Rawl. Often he would yell he had been slugged to hide his own foul play.

We were all in the room—a crowd of boys and girls. Rawl came in. He said: "Fee fo fum." I never knew any more until I arose perhaps five minutes afterwards. Rawl laughed and chewed his tobacco in the schoolhouse. I never said anything. There was nothing for me to say. I was weak. My eyes were blackened and my right eye was closed. I felt ashamed. That was the first time any fellow had ever done me like that. I wanted to sneak out and never come back to the school. That night when I was going home I was mad. I thought I ought to conceal a pistol on me and walk up and shoot Rawl down.

I told my father about the way it had happened. He said, "You are big enough to take care of yourself. But no man would ever do me that away." But I wouldn't kill Rawl, I concluded. It was weeks before the black rings left from under my eyes. I could hear people in the town saying: "There goes that boy John Briswell's boy hit. They said he shore beefed him. Hit him right under the eye and the next thing that Stuart boy knowed they's a-pouring water on him. I tell you John's got a bad boy. He'll go to the pen if he don't mind out—that boy will." Then flashes of madness would return to me and I would want to kill Rawl Briswell. At least I made up my mind to hit him and hit him hard. "Always get a man the first lick. That does the work. Hit him hard too. Stand on your toes and throw your weight behind your fist. Hit him hard the first time. That's the way your Uncle Rank always did."

When I went home that night I got a coffee sack out of the corn crib. I went up in the gap and filled the bottom of it with many pounds of sand. I took it inside the smoke house and fastened it to the pole where we had kept the middlings hanging. Then I took a brush and drew the nearest likeness of Rawl's face I could. I made a long mouth like he had with corners that dropped. He had a big mouth and I made a big mouth on the sack. That afternoon when I came home I practiced hitting that face with my fists. I would try it with a left and then a right. I was trying to get where I could swing the sack over the pole with my fist. This was in the spring of the year. One day a crowd of us were in the same schoolroom where I got hit by Rawl. Rawl was in the room. He started to say "Fee fo fum—" but before he had said his battle song I drove a left into the flesh of Rawl Briswell's face he'll long remember. As he was sinking to the floor I followed it with a right to his left jaw. The girls in the room began to scream. The boys closed the windows and held the door—so that there would be no excitement. Rawl came to himself in a room filled with students who were wishing that the two licks had been fatal ones. "Did you hear about that Stuart boy beefing that Briswell boy? It took the wad of tobacco out of his mouth and that was the whitest boy I've ever seen. He hit him hard enough to kill."

When Rawl came back to school with his eyes blacked, the teachers never said a word. They were glad it had been done, but they hadn't wanted to have the trouble of blacking his eyes. It was a greater task than teaching the school. I know I didn't want to do it at the cost of the lick he struck me. When he passed me in the schoolhouse one day he gritted his teeth and said: "I'll get you yet." I snapped, "Rawl, you won't get any boy your size. You won't get me. I'll whip you so quick you won't know that you are whipped." I determined to do it.

The last of the third year passed. I went back to the farm. One more year and I would finish school now. The summer before my senior year in high school I farmed another heavy crop. The new land on our farm was productive. During crop time I sat for the teachers' examination and got a second class certificate. That was good when only twenty-two passed out of forty-four and for one with twelve credits in high school. After the crops were laid by I went out and taught in a country school. Sixty-eight dollars a month beat making crossties and opossum hunting. It was easy-made money. I paddled a few girls for cursing and chewing tobacco behind the schoolhouse. The old women talked about that young man teacher putting young girls across his lap and using a book on them. "I don't think that is right to paddle a girl. He ought to take a willow switch and tickle her legs. I am afraid my man John will go around there to him if he paddles Jessie again." I had a great time with the hill children. I knew them. I was one. They didn't know it and I didn't tell them. I let the little children play all the time they didn't have to recite. It took play and association to make them keen and alert as well as it took books. They were starved for association. I turned them loose. It did them good. When I left there I gave the kids a bucket of mixed candy. It was their treat. Several of them cried and said: "We'll never see you again, Mr. Stuart." Well, they were right. I never went back.

When I returned to Greenup High School I had confidence in myself. I had nearly two hundred dollars now. I bought two new suits of clothes. I stepped out. I was a senior in high school now. I was invited to parties by the friends of Burl Mavis. When a substitute teacher was needed in mathematics or history, I filled the place. And time after time I served for days as a substitute teacher in the grades, making up my high school work at night. I played football that year and did some punting—something I liked very much to do. I was elected president of the Y.M.C.A. and of the Hi-Y club. I tied for the highest honors in my class. Burl Mavis had dropped from school now. He flunked his final exams when he was a junior. He went back to work in the store. The red-headed girl who had trouble saying *ring, rang* and *rung* was married.

That fall I went with hunting parties of town boys into the fields and woods near home. I would laugh and be gay with the crowd. I could laugh as loud as any of them, shoot as well and hunt better than most of them. We would go from field to field and not get any rabbits. I would say: "I must kill a rabbit. Don't anybody speak to me. Don't anybody follow me. I am afraid I may shoot you." I knew I wouldn't shoot one but I wanted silence. I would look for the rabbits' ears around stumps, in leaf beds and up against little clay banks. I would get down and look up under the edges of turf where the dirt was sliding down. I would see a rabbit. I would take the gun quickly and clip off its head. I found them that way. I never trusted trying to find a rabbit by looking for his tail. His tail is too often under the leaves. The ears were the things. Then the tail would fool one so often. Life everlasting has gray-looking leaves and tops that look like a rabbit's tail. I would explain to the boys how I found them. But it was not in many of them to know how to hunt. You know, I think a lot of these things are born with us. The first time I ever went into the hills hunting I killed two rabbits. I stole silently through the brush and found them. I found them for my father. Once I saw a rabbit crouched beside a stump fifty feet away. I went to the house, got the gun, and killed the rabbit. My father stepped the distance. "You have an eye for finding rabbits a-setten. I was never like that."

My high school days were over now. I had walked the eight miles per day with ease but during my senior year I stayed one third of my time in Greenup. I was a welcome member of many families. "You know right where the bed is. Now come any time and make yourself at home," said Mrs. Darby. "The key will always be above the door. Remember you are welcome here."

Now what was there for me to do? I was out of school. Must I go back to the farm? I remembered that on a snowy day in April 1918 I had broken a path for myself through the snow. I would not step in my father's broken path. I had said that I would not live among the hills forever and die among them and go back to the dust of the hills like my brothers had. I said my father would live his life among them and his life would be an empty life. He would give all of himself to the hills and in the end the hills would take him back and protect his bones against the elements. And briars and trees would soon cover his grave and the dead leaves from the trees would soon hide the prints of his grave. Now must I follow the footprints of my father? "Son, I'm in debt for part of this land yet. I'd like for you to go ahead with the work this summer. You know I am not able to hire help and James is too small to plow."

I thought it over. I told him I would stay for a while. But all the time I thought of the vows I had made to my mother at the milk gap. One day we took the mules to Greenup. It was the last time they were to see our farm. It was the last time I would follow them in the plow. We traded them for a team of horses. "Horses can stand up on this land now. It is pretty well worn and there are not many roots in it. Horses are not so dangerous either. They're not half so bad at kicking as mules. I got a little afraid of that Barnie mule when I went to put hay in his manger by lantern light at night. Mules are bad to kick." But a mule hates to leave a place he has learned to love. He hates to leave a place where he has given the best of his strength to get ready the land for corn and tobacco each spring. We had been fighting for a home of our own. Why not keep one for the mules? We had moved from place to place getting farms in good condition; then we moved on and left them. Among those corn fields and tobacco fields we had left strength and youth. We moved on and left the land in better shape than we got it from the landlord. Now the mules moved on, older and with less strength maybe, to a new home and the land that they had given their strength to help get in shape went to the horses. "Ain't it funny that a horse in the hills gets a quarter a day for his work and the man gets seventy-five? The horse does more than the man. Ain't it a queer thing? Now you take these country roads, what could we do without horses?" said Uncle Rank Larks.

I would get on the fastest young horse and ride as fast as the wind. I tried to outrun the wind. I would ride the ridge roads— out under the oak trees and the pine trees. Fred would jump draw-bars and gates with me. I would laugh and say, "Do it again, Fred." One day Mom said: "Jesse, teach Mary and James to ride. Make them take it barebacked."

I put Mary and James on Kate. They rode barebacked. I would get in front with Fred and he would set the pace for Kate to follow. We would ride the ridges. We would go to Cedar Riffles. I would point out the house where I was born to them. No one lived there now and a skunk denned under the floor. Birds built their nests under the eaves. Tall weeds grew beside the shack. The roof was leaking. We would ride beneath the oak trees and the pines. I would let Fred jump gates. Then Kate would follow. At first the children screamed. Then they began to like it. "Them Stuart youngins is plum fools. I seed them back over yander from Morton's Gap jist a raising hell with them horses. That little girl was with 'em. If them was youngins of mine, I'd whip their tails with a hickory," said old John Hackless.

But we worked hard in the fields together. We played hard together. But things to me were not what they once were. I dreamed of something beyond the hills. I wanted to go and go and go. I wanted to do something.

One night I was sitting in the chip yard talking to my father. I told him fifty acres of land was not a big enough place for me. He sat silently and gazed at a bunch of hollyhocks in the moonlight.

The Thread That Runs So True

IN HIS BOOK *Jesse Stuart* (New York: Twayne, 1968), Ruel Foster writes, "For years—since 1937, in fact—a book had been tumbling over and over in Stuart's head. More than anything else he wanted to write a book about teaching—a book that would be a song, a poem, a manifesto, a hymn to the profession of teaching" (26). In 1940 Stuart set out to write an article on teaching for *Progressive Farmer*. Realizing he had too much to say for an article, he tried writing a fictitious account that might help the South reduce the rate at which teachers were leaving for the North. It was apparently this manuscript that he took up again in January of 1948 when he became convinced of the necessity of writing a factual account based on personal experience. Dramatic in form, *The Thread That Runs So True* spans ten years of Stuart's life beginning with his first teaching job at seventeen and ending with his marriage to Naomi Deane Norris. Stuart planned to call his finished book *The Needle's Eye* because the teacher is the thread that holds a school together, but he chose the second line of an old play-song sung by mountain children instead:

> The needle's eye that does supply
> The thread that runs so true,
> Many a beau, have I let go
> Because I wanted you.
>
> Many a dark and stormy night,
> When I went home with you,
> I stumped my toe and down I go,
> Because I wanted you.

The book consists of six parts, each taking its title from a line of the song.

Late in 1948 Stuart completed his book and took part of the manuscript to New York to show the editors at Dutton in February of 1949, but Dutton did not publish it. Instead, *Ladies' Home Journal* published a condensed version in May, and on 26 September 1949, *Thread* was published by Scribners.

In *Jesse Stuart: His Life and Works* (Columbia: Univ. of South Carolina Press, 1967), Everetta Love Blair writes, "Stuart does not cling to his ivory tower, . . . but comes to grips with the hard realities of our times, and, in his works of social criticism, reflects the vital and wholehearted attention he has given to his areas of interest, particularly the field of education" (259). When it appeared, reviewers applauded *Thread* as a significant work of social criticism. Although an anonymous reviewer thought Stuart departed from the facts too much (*New Yorker*, 22 October 1949), and another thought *Thread* repetitious and monotonous (*Harper's*, November 1949), reviews were overwhelmingly positive.

Bill Bedell liked Stuart's faith in America and compared the Kentucky writer's ideals to those of Lincoln, Sandburg, Wolfe, and Roosevelt (*Houston Post*, 29 September 1949). A.J. Beeler referred to *Thread* as "a kind of sermon" (*Louisville Courier-Journal*, 2 October 1949), and Jesse Burt described it as an eloquent statement on the values of teaching (*Nashville Tennessean*, 9 October 1949). Harvey Ellis called the book "an ode to the Teaching Profession, the greatest of them all" (*Newark Star-Ledger*, 9 October 1949), and Thomas J. Fitzmorris referred to it as Stuart's "unblushing avowal to teaching" (*America*, 1 October 1949). Paul Flowers praised Stuart for not "tampering with sophistication" (*Memphis Commercial-Appeal*, 18 September 1949), and Kay Hamilton compared the way Dreiser, Lewis, and O'Hara would have written it to the way Stuart did (*Cincinnati Enquirer*, 1 October 1949). Daphne Alloway McVicker described it as a factual account "which rises to heights that are as epic as any Greek classic" (*Columbus Citizen*, 16 October 1949), and William McFee wrote that "here is revealed the essential greatness of America" (*Youngstown Vindicator*, 9 October 1949).

The following selection constitutes Part II of *The Thread That Runs So True*, which is included here not so much because it summarizes significant events in Stuart's life, but because it contains the Winston High School episode—one of the most inspirational stories about schoolteaching Stuart ever wrote.

"Jesse, we're so proud of you," Mom said, that Sunday in August I arrived home hitchhiking from Lincoln Memorial University. "We're proud to have a college graduate in our family. Larry Anderson is new Superintendent of Greenwood County Rural Schools. He's holding a good job for you!"

It had been five years since I had taught school in Lonesome Valley. During those five years I had finished my Senior year in Landsburgh High School. I had worked one year at the Auckland Steel Mills. I had worked up from "stand-by labor" to blacksmith. And I had finished college in three years. But I hadn't taken any educational courses at Lincoln Memorial to prepare myself for teaching. I had taken an academic course. I wanted to be the first of my people to finish college. I hadn't planned to teach school again.

For when I left the Auckland Steel Mills, I was ready to take over as a blacksmith. This would have paid me seven dollars a day. This wasn't as much money as Bill Coffee made, but with a college degree I had a chance to work up to something pretty good. I had read a newspaper account where one man had done this very thing. He had started with "stand-by labor" and had worked himself up to be president of a large steel company. If he could do this, I thought I could. I could work for the Auckland Steel Mills and earn money. I could invest this money in the company. I wouldn't spend it for an automobile too big to make the short turns in a narrow road.

I had made up my mind what I wanted to do the night I slept in a church house on my way home. A storm was coming up and I was walking along the highway. The lightning flashed and the thunder growled across the low, thin-bellied dark clouds. Darkness came suddenly. Several homes turned me down when I asked if I could spend the night. Then I walked and walked through the rain. But in a lightning flash I discovered the church house. The door was unlocked. I went inside and the lightning flashed until I could see the organ was covered. I took the cover from the organ and made myself a bed. While I lay on a seat, wrapped in the organ cover, watching the lightning flash around this old vine-covered church, I tried to come to some definite conclusions about my future. One of my decisions—one that was definite—was that I wouldn't teach school. I came to the final conclusion that I would return to the Auckland Steel Mills where a job was waiting for me. For America was on the boom, and the opportunities for a young ambitious man willing to work and to strive were unlimited. I knew this by experience.

I had hitchhiked to a small university I'd never heard of before, with twenty-nine dollars and thirty cents in my pocket, after I had been turned down by two colleges. I thought there was someplace that would take me. The college that Abraham Lincoln had asked General Howard to establish for "his people" accepted me.

I had worked my way through college. I had bought my books, clothes, paid my tuition, room rent and board on the twenty cents an hour that I earned. I had done all sorts of work at Lincoln Memorial. I had helped dig and lay water lines from the side of one mountain and across another; I had cleaned manholes and unstopped sewers, had mown grass over every foot of the spacious campus many times, had worked on the farm and at the dairy barn. I had washed and dried dishes, delivered mail, and for one year dried the pots and pans. I had my classes arranged so I could work one half of each day. And I had worked on the Bull Gang at the limestone quarry, where we blasted limestone rocks from beneath the roots of its cedar groves in Powell's Valley, broke them with sledge hammers (I was an expert with a sledge hammer for I had been a striker in the blacksmith-shop at the Auckland Steel Mills), then crushed them into slag for the Tennessee Highway Department. There was scarcely any kind of work at Lincoln Memorial I hadn't done. There wasn't any kind of work there I couldn't do. And all the outside financial help I had ever received were the two one-dollar bills my mother had sent to me. I had left Lincoln Memorial, hitchhiking home, with ten dollars in my pocket. I owed the school one hundred dollars. I had made better than B average.

Now I was home, surrounded by my people. There was rejoicing because I'd finished college. They were proud of me. At this time, Greenwood County with an approximate population of twenty-three thousand inhabitants, had less than a half-dozen native-born college graduates. Superintendent Larry Anderson had done some college work but he didn't have his degree.

"Mom, I've made up my mind to go back to the Auckland Steel Mills," I said. "I love to teach school. But remember my salary at Lonesome Valley?"

"Son, with all your education," my father said, "you can get in on the ground floor for something good in Greenwood County. You'll make more money now since you're a college graduate. Go see Larry about the job he's holdin' for you!"

"Yes, go see him at once, Jesse," Mom approved. "You know I don't want you to go back to the steel mills!"

"First of my people since they left Wytheville, Virginia, to get a college education," my father said. "They left Wytheville before the Civil War. I don't know what there was among my people before then."

"First college graduate among my people," Mom said proudly. "And I want you to do what my grandfather, Preston Hylton, did. I want you to teach school. I want you to teach school," she repeated. "I'm proud of you, Jesse. You're goin' to amount to something. They'll know you all over this county before long. Go see Larry Anderson at once. Go tomorrow!"

Monday morning when Larry Anderson came to unlock his office door, I was waiting.

"You're Jesse Stuart, aren't you?" he said, gripping my hand.

"Yes, sir," I said.

"Come in the office," he invited me. "I've been talking to your father about you. I've got a good place for you. You're the right man for the place. See," he explained, "I'm trying to do something for the Greenwood County Schools. I'm trying to do something with the amount of money we have to spend. I have school busses to haul pupils to Landsburgh High School in the east end of this county, and I have school busses to haul them to Maxwell High School in the west end. But we have approximately thirty-two miles of hard road over which our busses run. The rest is dirt road. And beyond where our busses can go are great spaces where the rural pupils haven't a chance to pass beyond the eighth grade. Not unless their parents are able to board their children near a high school. I have established three rural high schools in this county. I plan to send you to the Winston High School. Since we cannot get these pupils to our large high schools, I'm sending teachers to them."

"Who'll be on the faculty at the Winston High School?" I asked.

"You'll be all the faculty," he smiled. "You'll have fourteen pupils. Your salary will be one hundred dollars a month."

For a moment I sat thinking. In Landsburgh High School I had argued against taking algebra, Latin, and plane geometry. I had once said to Superintendent Herbert that these subjects should not be required. I'd gone even further. I'd said they should not even be taught. I had told him that I would never use them. He replied that everything I learned from my high-school subjects would have some value to me sometime in my life. The reason I argued against these subjects was that I failed Latin and plane geometry, and "got by" algebra by the skin of my teeth.

"What subjects will I have to teach at Winston High School?" I asked.

"Algebra, Latin, plane geometry, history, and English," he said.

"I'm afraid I can't teach algebra," I said.

"You've got mighty good college marks in algebra," he reminded me. "I have a transcript of your credits here! That's one reason I'm holding this high school for you. You fit the schedule. We don't have to warp the schedule to fit you."

I couldn't tell Superintendent Larry Anderson I had for my roommate at Lincoln Memorial, Mason Dorsey Gardner, who had won the coveted award of twenty-five dollars for being the best math student. I couldn't tell him Gardner had worked my algebra and I had written his themes.

"I'll take Winston High School," I said. "I'll be the faculty."

Saturday afternoon in early September I caught the Reo Speed Wagon that carried mail and passengers. I was on my way to Winston High School. I had a suitcase with my belongings. I had with me school supplies allotted a rural school. The Speed Wagon was packed with passengers. Women were sitting on men's laps, and children were sitting on the floor and the mailbags. There was a roof over us to keep the sun from blazing down upon our heads. There wasn't anything around us to keep away the wind and dust. Clouds of dust rose up behind us. When the Speed Wagon slowed down, the dust clouds swirled in behind and nearly choked us. We rode over the winding trail like a stagecoach

in an earlier day. But we went much faster. This was the only
communication line between Landsburgh and Winston.

We followed the Sandy River and then we went up Raccoon
and over a mountain and down into Hinton Valley. Then we
climbed another mountain, and, when we reached the top I saw
before me, deep down, one of the prettiest valleys I had ever
seen. The Tiber River wound slowly through the fertile farm
lands like a silver ribbon in the sunlight. We went down this east
wall of the valley, around the curves and up until we came to a
store and post office. This was Winston. This was where I got off
the Speed Wagon. I saw only one schoolhouse. This was the
Winston Rural School. But I was not looking for the schoolhouse
now. I was going to Baylors'—the big white house overlooking
the Tiber River. I saw the house in the distance. This was the place
where I would room and board.

That afternoon after Lucretia Baylor had shown me to my
room, Snookie and Robin Baylor, two pupils whom I would have
in Winston High School, went with me to show me the high-
school building. Though I had seen this dilapidated little building
when I passed by on the Speed Wagon, I didn't dream it was the
high school. This squat, ugly little structure had once been used
as a lodge hall. The lodge had been dissolved twenty years ago,
but the hall still stood though tumbling to decay. When I walked
inside a bat barely missed my head in its flight to escape. There
were wasps' nests, mud-daubers' nests, and birds' nests above
the window. A mavis flew from the nest through a broken win-
dowpane in her escape to freedom.

I walked outside. I wanted to inspect the outdoor privies and
the playground. Of all the thousands of acres of land there were
in this spacious broad valley, I had less than one sixteenth of an
acre for my high-school pupils. There was an outdoor privy in
each corner of this tiny lot. Horseweeds grew as tall as the
lodgehouse roof. The community's obscene artists had found
these privies. I sent Snookie back to the Baylors' to get water,
broom, scrub brush, soap, and a scythe.

That afternoon I went to work with two good helpers. We
cleaned the lodge hall. We scrubbed ceiling, walls, and floor. We
washed the walls of the privies. I scythed the small yard and
raked the horseweeds from the lot. Then I hacked down the sharp
stubble with a hoe. Snookie, Robin, and I put the schoolhouse,

the privies, and the yard in order. We were ready for school on Monday morning.

While we were working on the yard, a tall boy swaggered up the road and stopped. He stood there silently watching us. His hair was long. His face was pimpled. He had elongated blue eyes that squinted brightly when he looked at us. His loose-fitting clothes looked as if they would fall from his body.

"Hiya, Budge." Snookie spoke as soon as he saw him standing watching us.

"Hi are you, Snook?" Budge said.

"Comin' to school Monday, Budge?" Robin asked.

"Yep, I wouldn't miss it," he said.

"Here's your teacher," Snookie introduced us. "Mr. Stuart, this is Budge Waters."

"Glad to know you, Budge," I said. I'd never seen a youth in my life that looked anything like him. I'd never seen one with his peculiar actions when he walked. He used his hands to pull against the wind. This strange youth stood silently watching us work a few minutes. Then he walked away, swaggering as he walked and pulling the air with his hands.

"Are you kidding me about this fellow?" I asked Snookie. "Is he really a high-school pupil?"

"I'm telling you the truth," Snookie said. "He'll be the first one here Monday morning. He'll be here by daylight."

"How faraway does he live?" I asked.

"About seven miles," Snookie said.

"Doesn't he have any work to do at home?" I asked.

"Plenty of work," Snookie said. "They grow about ten acres of tobacco every year. They raise corn and cane too. Old Budge is a good worker."

"He might be a good worker," I agreed, "but he's going to find it hard to get through high school!"

"Don't you worry, Mr. Stuart," Snookie warned me. "If you're not awfully smart, he'll be teaching you!"

Monday morning when Snookie, Robin, and I got to school—an hour before time to start—twelve pupils were waiting, and I got the surprise of my life. Not one was barefooted. They were well dressed too. All but Budge Waters. His clothes were new and clean but they didn't fit his angular body too well. There was one

new automobile parked near the school. There were two handsome saddle horses tied in the shade of an elm tree. And there
was one pony almost as pretty as Sundance tied to the schoolyard
fence. The pupils came up and introduced themselves before we
started school. There were six girls and eight boys. Before time for
school to begin, I was acquainted with them and knew their
names.

Their schedule was already written on the small blackboard.
During my first day I gave them assignments, and we discussed
briefly the beginning lessons. With fourteen pupils and five
classes, each forty-five minutes long, I had a little time on my
hands. It was not like teaching at Lonesome Valley, where I had
fifty-four classes each day. During our brief discussions I realized
these Tiber Valley pupils would not be as easy to teach as my
pupils in Lonesome Valley had been. When I taught at Lonesome
Valley, I had completed my third year of high school and was only
three years ahead of my eighth-graders. But in training and general knowledge, there was a wide gap between us. I was eight
years ahead of my Winston High School pupils, and I had
thought, when I took this school, there would be a wide gap
between us.

When I started teaching ancient history I found one pupil who
knew more facts about this subject than I did. He was Budge
Waters. He went back to the beginning of the Pharoah kings of
Egypt; he named the kings, gave the dates in history when each
served, and told what each did for his country. I asked Budge if he
had taken this subject before. He told me he hadn't but he had
read all of his textbooks except algebra that summer. He said
algebra was hard for him, the other subjects were easy. Then I
asked him to read two paragraphs in his history book and when
he had finished I asked to hold his book. Then I asked him to tell
me what he had read in these paragraphs. While he told what he
had read I followed him in the paragraphs. He quoted the book
almost verbatim. Now I knew Snookie Baylor had told me the
truth! I asked Budge to read three more pages of history aloud to
the class and then tell me how much he had gotten from three
pages. Again, he almost quoted three pages. I had heard of
photographic memories. This was it. This boy didn't forget,
either. He had a retentive memory.

During my first week at Winston High School I knew my

problem was keeping ahead of these pupils, teaching them the subjects that had been hard for me in high school. I had to go home and work long hours in the evenings. I had to know my lessons. If I didn't, my pupils taught me. They did their assignments, no matter how much I gave them. The amount of work I gave them depended upon how much I wanted to study ahead. I had to study ahead in algebra, Latin, and plane geometry. I had to review my history and English too. I had to prepare five subjects.

I had accepted Winston High School, thinking it was a little place among the hills where my pupils would be the products of rural districts like Lonesome Valley. I had brought along a number of books to read so I wouldn't get lonesome. I wanted to have something to do. I found that I had plenty to do. I had to work to keep ahead of Budge Waters. He remembered dates better than I. When we had disagreed on dates, we looked them up in the encyclopedia, and Budge Waters was always right. Where did this boy get all his knowledge? Where did the other thirteen get their information too? Who were these pupils? What was their background? I was faced with one of the strangest problems I had ever known a teacher to have. And here was the place I would least expect to find such a problem.

Nine of my fourteen pupils came from farms. The sales of farm products were their total earnings. Billie Leonard, who rode the pony nine miles to school, was the son of a coal miner. Another was the son of a rural teacher, who supplemented his salary by farming during the summer. And I had the son and daughter of a deputy county sheriff. He had farmed before he was appointed deputy sheriff. Not one of the parents of my pupils was a college graduate. Not one had ever been to college. Not one was a high-school graduate. The rural teacher had only a few credits in high school. The majority of them hadn't finished grade work in the rural schools. But these parents had another kind of education. They knew the soil they farmed. They knew what to plant, where to plant, and when to plant. They knew how to cultivate their land. They had learned these things by experience. And they knew when and how to harvest.

While the men worked with the soil and the seasons, their thrifty wives ran their homes. There was some contrast to the homes in Tiber Valley and in Lonesome Valley. The reason for these differences perhaps was the soil. The Tiber River soil was better than the Lonesome Valley soil. And the Tiber Valley farmers used newer methods of farming, better machinery, and they cared for their land. This land to them was something like their own flesh and blood. Their forefathers, approximately a century and a half before, had settled in this valley. The same names, same families, same blood streams were here. With the passing of the years, the farms had grown smaller. They had been divided by the children when their elders died, divided again and again until the farms had not great boundaries they once had. Each cliff, forest, stream, and large roadside tree had some affectionate meaning to them.

During crop season if one man got behind with his work, or if he had sickness in his family and couldn't work, his neighbors helped him. It was the same in autumn harvest. The people worked in unison. They helped each other. There were no feuds. They were good neighbors. There were four different religious denominations. There were as many churches. Not anyone was particularly interested in what church you attended. That was your business. If you didn't attend a church at all, you weren't criticized. And everybody, in the different churches, aimed at the same heaven. This was hard for me to believe after my experience at Lonesome Valley, which was less than thirty miles away.

Of the thirty-two voting precincts in Greenwood County, Winston was the only precinct where neither of the two major political parties could use money. They didn't even attempt to buy votes at Winston. Each political party could almost count the Winston vote before it was cast. Usually there was a tie vote. At least, neither party ever carried the precinct with more than seven votes. Often the majority either way would be one or two votes. These people were the parents of the pupils I was teaching in Winston High School. These were the old landlocked Americans for whom Superintendent Larry Anderson had established a high school to give their children more educational opportunities. Their children were willing to take advantage of any opportunities.

At the end of my first two weeks I knew I was learning algebra, Latin, and plane geometry. I didn't worry about my pupils. All I worried about was keeping ahead of them. I thought I might ease the situation and not have to work so hard myself if I brought them more books to read. We didn't have a library. We had only a dictionary and an encyclopedia. The books I had brought to read myself, my pupils read in the first two weeks. And'they were asking for more books. Budge Waters didn't read by sentence. He read by paragraph.

That was the reason on the Saturday morning of my second week I caught the Speed Wagon for Landsburgh. From Landsburgh, I walked five miles home. I didn't have any way to get back to Winston on Sunday. The Speed Wagon didn't carry mail on Sunday. I might be lucky enough to catch a ride after I walked from W-Hollow to the Sandy River Turnpike. I would have a heavy load of books to carry a long distance. But I didn't mind carrying books to pupils as eager to read as my Winston High School pupils.

I didn't know the kind of books to select for these pupils. There was an "age level of books" recommended for high-school Freshmen, but I didn't know about it. I filled my suitcase with books I loved. Books, I thought, that would keep them reading for some time. I chose books by Tolstoy, Melville, Chekhov, Victor Hugo, De Maupassant, Balzac, Thomas Hardy, Sinclair Lewis, Emerson, Whittier, Hamlin Garland, Dreiser, Whitman, Poe, Edgar Lee Masters, Bret Harte, and Jack London. With my suitcase full, I followed a fox path across the Seaton Ridge to the Sandy River Turnpike, which was three miles closer than if I had gone by Landsburgh. I walked up the dusty turnpike along the river, then up Racoon Valley and over the mountain. I walked down into the Hinton Valley and up to the top of the east wall overlooking the Tiber Valley. I put my suitcase down and was resting under the shade of a roadside tree. I had walked about eleven miles with a forty-pound load. I was sweaty and tired. Then a stranger with an Ohio license on his car drove up, stopped, and asked me to ride. He took me all the way to Winston.

Monday I introduced my pupils to these new authors. I told them to take the books, read them, and exchange them until everybody had read them. I told them they were my books. All I wanted them to do was to take care of them and return them when they were through. Budge Waters selected *War and Peace.*

My getting novels, books of poetry, essays, and short stories didn't keep my pupils from crowding me. How I wished that I had worked harder in high school and college! How I wished that

I had learned everything in my assignments! I had thought I would never use this subject matter again. All I hadn't learned, I was having to learn. All I had learned and had tried to forget, I was having to review. And this kept me busy. This was the first time in my life I had ever heard of high-school pupils crowding their teacher. It had always been the other way around. This made me wonder if I had been a good forgetter of all I had learned, or if I hadn't learned at all.

Since I had had only two years of Latin and was now trying to teach first-year Latin, I had to spend considerable time on this subject. And by doing this, I neglected to work ahead of my pupils in algebra. One day in the third week, Billie Leonard came up to me, and said, "Mr. Stuart, will you show me how to work this algebra problem?"

I looked at the problem. It was a problem about trains starting at given points and running toward each other so many miles per hour and how long would it be before they met. I had never solved this problem in my first-year algebra.

"Billie, I can't work this problem," I laughed, telling him the truth.

"Mr. Stuart, I understand," he answered. "You want your pupils to work these problems, don't you?"

"Yes, if they can," I said.

In less than thirty minutes Billie Leonard was back with the problem solved. He showed it to me.

"Your theory is right, Billie," I said. "You've solved this problem."

I knew he was right after I had seen it worked. But Billie Leonard never knew that I couldn't actually work this problem. Often my pupils solved algebra problems before I could. I threw the responsibility of plane geometry, algebra, and Latin directly upon them. I was just a little-better pupil in plane geometry and Latin working along with them. In the subject of algebra, I doubt that I was as good as half the members of the class. But the way we covered algebra and the way my pupils learned it gave me another thought. I wondered if many teachers weren't too good in the subjects they taught and if they didn't teach over their pupils' heads. This experience made me wonder if it wasn't better when the teacher didn't know his subject too well and had to work with his pupils closer. Then he had more sympathy and understanding.

Budge Waters had a strange sense of humor. He never laughed unless one of his classmates made a mistake. And they made mistakes. When he laughed he laughed all over. His whole body shook. And when his teacher made a mistake, he would laugh until tears came from his elongated eyes and ran down his pimpled cheeks. He would laugh until all his classmates and his teacher would start laughing at him. His teacher did considerable laughing too.

When I had first come to Winston, I wondered what my pupils did for recreation. I wondered what I would do for recreation. I had thought reading was about the only kind of recreation. It didn't take me long to learn differently. One evening in September I was invited to Bill Madden's home. He was one of my pupils. His father had invited six or seven of the local musicians in to play for us. We sat in the yard where the grass was dying and the peach-tree leaves had turned golden and the moon was high in the sky above us. We listened to this local band play with their banjos, fiddles, guitar, mandolin, and accordion from seven until eleven. They never played the same tune twice, and often when they played a fast breakdown, one of the listeners would dance. I had never heard old-time music sound as beautiful as this, in the moonlight of the mild September evening.

There was hardly a family in this big vicinity who didn't have a musician. This was part of their recreation. People had learned to play musical instruments to furnish their own music just as they had learned to plant, cultivate, and harvest crops for their food supply. They depended upon themselves for practically everything.

I went with my pupils, their parents, and neighbors to cornhuskings, apple-peelings, bean-stringings, square dances, and to the belling of the bride when there was a wedding. Often we rode mules many miles through darkness or moonlight to these community events. I never missed a party at the mill when they made sorghum molasses in this great cane country. We went to the sorghum mill, shoved each other in the skimmings-hole and ate the soft sweet foam from the boiling cane juice with long paddles whittled from willow wood. I went to all of the churches. I went with my pupils to the churches of their choice. I went to parties where we played post office and where we danced Skip to my

Lou. . . . I didn't worry about recreation. I found plenty of recreation. It was the kind of recreation in which the old, middle-aged, and young took part. There were not a few having fun and a whole crowd around them to watch. This was the most democratic recreation I had ever seen.

Not one of my pupils had ever seen a stage play. If one had ever seen a movie, I'd never heard of it. They didn't have to leave landlocked Winston to find recreation. They had it at home. They created it just as they created most of their necessities of life. As the autumn days wore on they popped corn over the blazing wood fires and made molasses-and-popcorn balls. There was somewhere to go every night. I couldn't accept all the invitations. Each pupil invited me to his home to spend the night. This was an old custom, for in the past years the teacher had boarded with his pupils since his salary wasn't enough to enable him to pay his board and have anything left.

When the hunting season came I hunted quail with my pupils. I hunted rabbits with them in the Tiber weed fields. My pupils were good marksmen. But I gave them a few surprises at some of the shots I made. I had never told them about my years of hunting experience. I went to the autumn-coloring hills to hunt possums. And I taught them—as I had tried to teach them high-school subjects—a little about possum hunting: that on the still and misty, warm nights when not a leaf stirred was the time to catch possums and coons. When I learned more about the terrain of the east and west walls, where the persimmons and pawpaws grew, I showed them where to find the possums. They—as I had once done—hunted for animal pelts, shipped them, and bought books and clothes with the money. I showed them how to take better care of their pelts.

Many nights I climbed with them to the top of the east or west wall with a pack of hounds. Often there were twenty-five or thirty men with us and we'd have from thirty to fifty hounds to chase the fox. We'd build a fire on the highest peak of stone or earth and listen to the music of the running hounds. We could hear the music of their barking, for we were high enough to listen to them circle the fox around us. We braved all sorts of weather to listen to the magic barking and running of the hounds. On many a moon-light night we saw the fox not more than a hundred yards ahead of the speckled, black, white, brown-and-tan hounds as they came pouring from the autumn woods into an open field with their heads high in the air. The fox was hot and left much scent on the wind. The hounds didn't have to put their noses to the earth. They could smell the fox ahead instead of nosing the earth for his track.

Then came the autumn rains when the Speed Wagon no longer made the mail run to Landsburgh. The only road that connected the valley with the county-seat town was impassable. Anybody wanting to go to Landsburgh had to provide his own means of transportation. He had to walk, ride muleback or horseback, or take two teams hitched to one wagon. For the valley—after the autumn rains, after the freezes and thaws—became a sea of mud. The slender, winding road was a ribbon of mud. I saw loads of tobacco leaving Winston with as many as three mule teams hitched to one wagon. I never saw a wagon loaded with barrels of sorghum or tobacco have less than two mule teams. It took one good mule team to pull an empty wagon; the wheels sank in mud to their hubs. Winston was isolated. This was why the people depended upon themselves for everything. When the Speed Wagon stopped making the run to Landsburgh, people knew the long winter months of isolation had begun.

The mail was carried by horseback. Wid Maddox put his Speed Wagon away to use again next May or June, depending on the condition of the roads. The people in Winston knew spring had returned when the Speed Wagon started hauling mail. Now Wid used from four to six horses. He rode one and led a pack horse. When the mail was heavy, he often led two pack horses. He rode part of the thirty-odd-mile mail route to where he put these horses in a barn at "midway." There he got fresh horses and continued his journey to Landsburgh. He spent the night in Landsburgh. Next morning he rode to midway, where he exchanged his tired horses for fresh ones so he could continue his journey over the ribbon of sloppy mud.

When the leaves changed color in the valley and the sun was bright as a brush-pile flame, I went on long hikes with my pupils. We'd take a hike to the autumn-colored hills soon as the school day was over. We'd take food to cook over an open fire on the summit of one of the walls that enclosed the valley. Sometimes the girls would go with us. The hike to the highest summits was often a strenuous climb. We would see the valley below in its autumn colors while we ate and talked.

The Tiber Valley walls grew mostly one type of tree. That was the tough-butted white oak. This tree choked almost all other types of growth on these infertile slopes. It would root well into the hard, bony earth and into the rock crevices, and in autumn when these leaves colored they were beautiful to see. On each side of the valley, these leaf-clouds rose toward the sky until they reached the pine groves on the walls' crests. These leaf-clouds were brilliant when they rippled in the sun. The pine groves made green clouds between the golden leaf-clouds and the blue of the sky.

Down in the valley we could see every splash of color. Green leaves were there still, for the Tiber mists had protected them against the biting frost. There were blood-red shoe-make leaves, golden sycamore and poplar leaves, slate-colored water-birch leaves, and the dull- and bright-gold willow leaves. And down in the valley the corn shocks stood like wigwams in an Indian Village. We could see the bright knee-high corn stubble glittering in the autumn sun. We could see the brown meadow stubble, too, where the hay had been mown and piled in high mounds with poles through the center.

Often I walked alone beside the Tiber in autumn. For there was a somberness that put me in a mood that was akin to poetry. I'd watch the big sycamore leaves zigzag from the interlocking branches above to the clear blue Tiber water and drift away like tiny golden ships. I'd find the farewell-to-summer in bloom along this river. Then a great idea occurred to me. It wasn't about poetry. It was about schools.

I thought if every teacher in every school in America—rural, village, city, township, church, public, or private—could inspire his pupils with all the power he had, if he could teach them as they had never been taught before to live, to work, to play, and to share, if he could put ambition into their brains and hearts, that would be a great way to make a generation of the greatest citizenry America had ever had. All of this had to begin with the little unit. Each teacher had to do his share. Each teacher was responsible for the destiny of America, because the pupils came under his influence. The teacher held the destiny of a great country in his hand as no member of any other profession could hold it. All other professions stemmed from the products of his profession.

Within this great profession, I thought, lay the solution of most of the cities', counties', states', and the nation's troubles. It was within the teacher's province to solve most of these things. He could put inspiration in the hearts and brains of his pupils to do greater things upon this earth. The schoolroom was the gateway to all the problems of humanity. It was the gateway to the correcting of evils. It was the gateway to inspire the nation's succeeding generations to greater and more beautiful living with each other; to happiness, to health, to brotherhood, to everything!

I thought these things as I walked in the somber autumn beside this river and watched the leaves fall from the tall bank-side trees to the blue swirling water. And I believed deep in my heart that I was a member of the greatest profession of mankind, even if I couldn't make as much salary shaping the destinies of fourteen future citizens of America as I could if I were a blacksmith with little education at the Auckland Steel Mills.

Nobody could keep me from starting home. I was determined to go. I needed more novels, books of short stories, books of poems and essays for my pupils to read. I wanted to see Superintendent Larry Anderson. When Lucretia Baylor learned I was determined to go, she prepared a quick hot lunch for me. She did this while I packed my clothes and got ready. For my teaching day ended at 3:30 P.M., and I had walked the three-fourths mile to Baylors' in a hurry. It was early in the afternoon, but the dark December skies hung low over the valley, and there were six inches of snow on the ground. I had seventeen miles ahead of me. The only way I could get to my destination was to walk.

"If you were a boy of mine," Ottis Baylor said, "I wouldn't let you go. Not on a seventeen-mile journey on a night like this! I advise you against going. I know the road to Landsburgh better than you do. I've walked it enough to know. It's a treacherous road when you leave the Tiber Valley Road and try the short cut around Laurel Ridge."

I knew that I wasn't listening to Ottis Baylor. I was going, anyway. I knew that I was fast on foot. I had walked thirty-five miles in a day. That hadn't even made my legs or feet sore. If I could walk this far on a short day, then I was as positive as death, by steady walking, I could cover a mile every twelve minutes. I thought: If I had luck, I could make the journey in three and a half hours. I allowed myself four hours and that was plenty of time. And I was leaving Baylors' at four.

The massive black cloud rested on the east and west walls of the valley like a roof. The east wall was the one I had to climb. When I reached the top I would be on the Laurel Ridge. By going this way, I could cut three miles from my walking distance. I knew the path to Laurel Ridge. I'd been over it many times before. Whether the snow was broken over this path or not, I did not know. I did not care. I said good-bye to Baylors', and I was on my way.

The December wind whistled in the barren shoe-make tops, where the red birds hopped from limb to limb and chirruped plaintive notes. Snowbirds stood by the clumps of dead ragweed the snow hadn't covered. They were searching for a scanty supper of the frozen seeds. Though time was early on this short winter day, I thought darkness might come soon. Going up the mountain, I made excellent time. I followed the path all right. I had to break the snow, for no one had traveled this path. I knew how to follow the path by the clumps of trees, rock cliffs, and fences. These were the landmarks to follow. When the path was covered in snow these landmarks still looked the same.

When I reached the big opening—a cleared cove where tobacco had been farmed—I knew I was halfway to Laurel Ridge. And from Baylors' to Laurel Ridge was approximately three miles. I looked at my watch and it had taken me thirty minutes. This was slower time than I had expected. The snow was even deeper high on the mountain. The path was harder to break. Ottis and Lucretia Baylor might have been right when they warned me against going but I would not turn back. I was going on even if I didn't get home before midnight. I was halfway to Laurel Ridge now. I saw a rabbit hop across my path, and when he saw me he took long hops for a saw-brier thicket. The rabbit thought night was here, for rabbits sleep on winter days and stir at night.

Before I reached the second small opening near Laurel Ridge, I lost my path. I walked into a forest of tough-butted white oaks. They grew close together shutting out the diminishing winter light. I had never seen these trees before. I turned quickly, retracing my steps until I found the path. I knew I had been in too much of a hurry. I'd have to be more careful. I'd not walked more than a hundred yards when a red fox, almost as big as a collie, crossed my path. When he saw me he took off with full speed and disappeared in the wintry dusk that was getting thicker on the mountain. I wondered now if I had reached the black cloud that seemed to rest there. I wondered if that was why the dusk was suddenly turning to darkness. But why should I worry now? I had at least reached Laurel Ridge, for there was a five-strand, rusty barbed-wire fence nailed to the trees. I knew this fence. It followed Laurel Ridge some distance before it turned back down the mountain. When I held my arm up to look at my watch, I couldn't see the figures on the dial. I didn't know what time it was, but I knew it was early. I knew I was in the snow cloud. For the big snowflakes were falling around me. I could see them dimly, these white flakes about the size of dimes, falling just in front of my eyes. I could feel them hitting my overcoat.

All I had to do was turn to my left after I reached Laurel Ridge. That was the right direction. I could follow the wire fence even if I had to follow it with my hand as I walked. I had one free hand. I carried my suitcase with my right hand. My left hand was free. But I didn't touch the fence. Not yet. I was following Laurel Ridge Road. I was following it with my feet. I had hunted much at night in my lifetime. Darkness had never bothered me too much. But now I couldn't see the woods and I knew it couldn't possibly be six o'clock. I was in a snowstorm. I could hear the snowflakes falling through the barren oak tops whose branches interlocked above the road.

Then I heard voices, and the sound was sweet to hear. I had barely time to side-step for two mule teams. I almost walked into a mule before I saw him. Yet there was a lighted lantern on the joltwagon the mules were pulling. When I recognized Eif Potters, he stopped his mule team in great surprise. He asked me where I was going on a night like this. Then I knew what he was talking about.

The fury of the storm almost blotted out the lantern light. It didn't give light more than six feet away. The snowflakes were larger than nickels. They were almost as large as quarters. I was in the cloud I'd seen before I left Baylors'.

I told Eif Potters and his son Zeke, who was sitting on the wagon beside him, I was on my way home. That snow wasn't falling down in Tiber Valley when I left, not more than two hours ago. He told me they hadn't been in the snowstorm until they reached the top of Raccoon Hill. Then he invited me to get on the wagon and go home with them, but I refused. When I refused he said he would loan me his lantern, but that they couldn't get around Laurel Ridge without it. Said he had five more miles to go, that he had taken a load of tobacco to Landsburgh and was getting back the same day, that he and his mules were very tired to push through five more miles of darkness and storm.

On this lonely ridge, high up in a snow cloud, I said good night to Eif and Zeke and was on my way, for I had lost about five minutes talking to them. I hadn't walked but a few steps when I looked back. The mule teams, wagon, riders, and lantern had disappeared in the storm. Yet I heard the jingling of the mules' harness, and I heard the men's voices as they talked to each other. Then I plunged on, alone, taking in both sides of the road. I hunted for the fence with an outstretched hand in the darkness, but I couldn't find it.

Eif had warned me about one place. He told me if I bore too far to my left I would go into a vast tract of timber that lay on the east wall of Timber Valley. And for this reason, I bore to my right, feeling with my feet while the snow came down as I had never felt it fall before. One thing I had forgotten to ask Eif for was matches. He was a pipe-smoker too. He had smoked his pipe all the time he sat on his wagon and talked to me. If only I had a match! I was stumbling over the road. Once I went in water to my knee. Then I knew I must be on the Laurel Ridge Road. This was a deep wagon-wheel rut, and Eif had driven over it and had broken the thin ice down to the water. My foot was wet. Water squashed in my shoe. One of my galoshes was filled with water.

Then I stepped into a hole of water with my dry foot. I went in to my knee. Both pant legs were wet to my knees. Again and again I stepped into water, but my feet were already wet and it didn't make any difference if I did get them wet again. I kept moving. I followed the road the best I could. I knew I was on the Laurel Ridge Road. That was the main thing. I would soon reach the turnpike at the top of Raccoon Hill. That was where the Laurel Ridge Road ended. And this distance was approximately three miles from where my path from Baylors' had gone through the barbed-wire fence onto the Laurel Ridge. If I could only see my watch! I had surely walked three more miles!

Time in the night, I thought, when one was walking alone, might seem longer than it actually was. I kept on going. I waded water, and I waded snow. The snow was almost as deep as my galoshes were high. I walked on and on and on. Then I knew I'd gone far enough to reach the turnpike on Raccoon Hill . . . the turnpike that would take me straight to Landsburgh. While I thought about the fast time I would be able to make on the turnpike when I reached it, I suddenly walked into a cornfield. I thought it was a cornfield. I thought I was standing beside a fodder shock. It stood like a white wigwam before me. I pushed my hand through the snow and felt the dry fodder stalks. I knew now that I was lost.

I couldn't even retrace my steps. I couldn't see them. If it had been light enough for me to see them, I couldn't have followed them far because they would have been snowed under. I was lost, that was all. I was in this cornfield and I would have to make the best of it. I stood beside the fodder shock—this tiny thing of security—while I screamed at the top of my voice. I knew that in this part of Greenwood County there was much wasteland. There were miles and miles where there wasn't a house. But I screamed, anyway. I thought somebody might hear me and come to my rescue. The only answer I got was the far-away barking of a fox. When I screamed he mocked me with his barking.

When I had reached this fodder shock, my feet were still warm and my face was wet with perspiration. But in this open space where corn had grown on the mountaintop there was an incessant sweep of wind. The wind carried the snow directly at me. I could measure the speed of the wind by the way the soft flakes hit my face. The soft flakes felt like grains of corn. I had to start walking to keep warm. I had to do something in a hurry. Then a thought came to me. If there was one fodder shock here, there were others. The cornfield must be fairly large to give the wind such great velocity. I was almost afraid to leave the fodder shock I had already found. Even when I did, I held to my suitcase. I walked a few paces and found another fodder shock. I put my arm around the top of the shock and dragged it back to the first one. I carried eight fodder shocks to one place. The fodder shocks were not large. The shocks were not as tall as I was. I used one hand to carry them; I held to my suitcase with the other. I was afraid I'd lose it and that it would soon be snowed under. Besides, I had other ideas.

After I'd pulled these fodder shocks together, I laid the heavy ends of the fodder to the windward side of the mountain. I bedded three shocks down on the snow. Then I put a shock on each side of the floor I'd made. I stood two shocks up on the windward side, to pull down on me as soon as I was ready to lie down. The last shock I stood up, to use where the fodder would be thinnest above me. Then I stood on the fodder and pulled off my shoes. The wind-driven snow was cold to my wet feet and legs. I pulled off my overcoat and wet pants. I took a dry soiled shirt from my suitcase and dried the water from my feet and legs. I tied dry dirty shirts around my feet. I put on a pair of soiled trousers I was taking to have dry-cleaned. I bundled myself with all the clothes I had in my suitcase. I lay down and spread my overcoat over me. Now I reached up and pulled the fodder shocks down upon me. The fodder quilt was thick but not too heavy. I lay there and listened to the mice in the fodder around me and the ticking of my watch while over me the wind moaned and the snow fell.

I knew that I should not go to sleep. For if I did the wind might blow the fodder from over me. I would freeze to death and I would not be found in this cornfield until the farmer came to haul his fodder home. I must have been half-asleep when I heard the hoot owls start calling to one another from the timber all around this cornfield. I didn't know exactly where they were. But I knew they frequented the less-populated places. From their calls, coming from all directions, I knew this must be their meeting place. I no longer heard the wind nor felt it seeping through the fodder. I parted the fodder stalks to see what had happened. There were a million bright stars high in the clear blue sky, and in a short distance all around me—for there was not more than two acres of this cornfield—I could see the dark outlines of trees. Among these trees were the hoot owls. They were on every side. They cried jubilantly to each other, asking always the same: "Who, who are you?"

I pulled the fodder quilt back over me and lay there listening to the hoots of the owls, to the mice over me, around me and through the fodder, and to the ticking of my watch. I thought that

I could stay awake until morning. Since the skies had cleared, I knew the weather before morning would be sub-zero on this mountaintop. I went to sleep dreaming that I would not go to sleep.

When I awoke there were fewer stars in the sky. Daylight didn't come on these short December days until nearly eight. I tried to see what time it was, but I couldn't see the hands of my watch. The owls had flown away, and all was silent save for the ticking of my watch and the mice that had never slept the whole night through. I had slept warm on this cold night. I had warmed the fodder for the mice. The place was comfortable for all of us. But now I sat up and placed the fodder around me like a wigwam. I wanted the day to break so I could put on my clothes and be on my way. I had never been so hungry in my life.

Just as soon as it was light enough to see what I was doing, I started dressing. The legs of the pants I'd pulled off were frozen stiff and hard. My shoes had frozen so that I couldn't get them on. I didn't have a match to build a fire to thaw them. It was impossible to put them on. I wrapped a soiled shirt around each foot. I put my feet into my frozen galoshes. I put my frozen shoes and pants into my suitcase. It was light enough for me to see dim footprints in the snow. I could retrace myself. I wanted to see where I had made my mistake.

I followed my tracks, dim little prints in the crusted snow, for more than a mile. Then I came to Laurel Ridge. Far, far, down below, I could see Hinton Valley, now a great white silence except for the dark, leafless, sleeping trees. And to my right, if I had gone just fifty feet to my left, I would have found the turnpike on Raccoon Hill. I had borne too far to my right after Eif Potters had warned me about turning left. I had gone somewhere on the mountain between the headwaters of North Fork and Raccoon, where I found the cornfield and slept in the fodder.

Though it was Saturday morning when farmers would be on their way to Landsburgh, I was the first person on the turnpike. The white silence of snow that was even with the tops of my galoshes remained unbroken until I made a path. I walked down Raccoon Hill, and in the distance, somewhere far down the road, I heard voices. They were coming toward me. I was going toward them. Their shouts at their teams grew louder. I saw three teams hitched to a snowplow and the county road-workers were breaking the road. I walked past them, and they looked at me. I hadn't noticed the fodder blades still hanging to my overcoat, and I brushed them off before I stopped at Gullet's gristmill.

I knew Ephraim Gullet. When I went inside the gristmill he asked me if I wasn't traveling early. I told him I had been lost and had slept on the mountain. He put more coal in the potbellied stove. He made a pot of coffee. I thawed my shoes and my pant legs while I drank hot coffee and warmed myself in front of the red-hot stove. Ephraim told me that his thermometer was twelve below at six that morning. He couldn't understand how I had stripped my clothes and dried the water from my legs and feet there on the mountaintop facing the great sweeps of snow-laden wind. He couldn't understand how I had managed to survive the rigor of the raw elements on the mountaintop when it was twelve below in the valley.

When Superintendent Larry Anderson unlocked his office door at nine that Saturday morning, I was there waiting for him. I had caught a ride in on a coal truck from Gullet's gristmill to Landsburgh.

"Well, well, how did you get here so early?" Superintendent Anderson asked. "You didn't come all the way from Winston this morning?"

"Just part of the way," I said.

He didn't ask me where I stayed. And I didn't tell him. I had something else I wanted to talk to him about.

"How are you getting along with your school out there?" he asked me.

"I'm getting along all right," I said. "What reports have you heard?"

"Good reports," he said.

"I'm glad to hear the reports about my teaching have been favorable," I said. "I am learning myself. My pupils are working me as hard as I am working them!"

My Superintendent thought I was joking. He started laughing. He laughed until he couldn't talk.

"I'm telling you the truth," I said. "I'm not telling you a joke. I've worked harder than I did in high school or in college!"

Superintendent Larry Anderson laughed harder than before.

He laughed so loud anybody in the corridors of the courthouse could have heard him.

"You know there's not anything as good for a man as a good laugh early in the morning," he said.

I knew that he still thought I was joking.

"Superintendent Anderson," I said seriously, "I'm up against teaching those fourteen pupils. I've not got a slow one among them. I've got a couple of average pupils, and they can do every bit of work I give them. And," I explained, with a gesture of my hand for emphasis, "I've got one pupil that's a genius. He knows more facts than I do. He's only a Freshman in high school. I tell you, Budge Waters is a genius! If he isn't, I'm terribly dumb. I've got six or seven A pupils and he's above them!"

"Do you grade by the curve system?" he asked.

"Certainly not," I said.

"Why not?" he asked.

"I didn't make a bad record in high school," I said. "I made better than B average in college. I have first-year high-school pupils crowding me. They ask me intelligent questions I cannot answer. Why should I string pupils like these over a curve system? Not any more than I should take a poor pupil from a group of poor ones and give him an A because he is a fraction better than the others!"

Superintendent Larry Anderson sat silently looking at me for a minute. We were in his office alone. No other rural teachers had reached Landsburgh. Then he spoke thoughtfully: "Well, what is your problem?"

"I haven't any," I said. "I've not had to discipline a pupil. They work hard. They play hard."

I knew he was wondering why I had come to his office.

"But there is one thing I'd like to do," I said. "That's why I've called on you this morning. I'd like to test my own judgment to see if I am wrong or right in my opinion of my pupils. I'd like to know how to go about entering them in the state scholastic contest. The contest is held each spring, isn't it?"

"Oh, yes," he said, "but there is an elimination process. Your pupils will have to take an examination against the pupils in Landsburgh High School! Then, if you are successful there," he explained, "they'll go to Auckland to enter the district contest. If they are successful there, they'll go on to the state contests!"

I knew that to get past Landsburgh, now a joint city-and-county high school, we'd have to compete with the best from nearly four hundred pupils. To get past the regional, we'd have to compete with the best, selected from thousands. Yet, it took only one brain to win a contest. I knew Budge Waters had that brain if it was properly trained. I thought he was capable of competing state-wide. I thought Billie Leonard could take the district in algebra. And I was willing to challenge big Landsburgh High School in all the five subjects I was teaching my pupils.

"If it's all right with you, Superintendent," I said, "you make arrangements and set a date for us to meet Landsburgh High School in algebra, Latin, English, plane geometry, and history!"

"I'll do it," he smiled. "Would sometime in January suit you?"

"Any time's all right with me," I said. "Make it convenient for the Landsburgh High School!"

"That's fair enough," he said.

"This is all I wanted to see you about," I said.

With these words, I left him alone in his office.

Sunday morning at nine o'clock I left W-Hollow for Winston. I walked briskly over the frozen snow that crunched beneath my feet. I faced the unmerciful December wind. It whipped my clothes. It stung my face. But I knew I would not get cold. For I was carrying a load of twenty books I had borrowed for my pupils. They had already read all of my books. I was also carrying a limited supply of clothes. I couldn't bring all the clothes I wanted to bring because the books occupied most of the space in my suitcase. I was on my way over the frozen snow, beneath a sunless sky, facing a terrific wind . . . and I would go all the way this time in daylight. I wouldn't make the mistake I'd made before. Despite the frigid wind, the sunless sky, the crunching, frozen snow, I was carrying a load that would keep me warm.

I took the near cut across the Seaton Ridge. This would save me three miles. And when I reached the Seaton Ridge, I had never faced such a biting wind as blew from the north. I was glad to get over the ridge and down to the Sandy River Turnpike. It was much warmer down in the Sandy River Valley. Here I had hopes of catching a ride. But I walked on and on along the slick turnpike. The road plows hadn't scooped away the ice on the road. It was still there. I never met a person on the Sandy River Turnpike.

Then I reached Raccoon. I walked all the way, hoping against hope that I would catch a ride. Though perspiration stood on my face, my body was chilled by the wind, and if I stopped thirty seconds the perspiration dried on my face.

When I reached the top of Raccoon Hill, I looked at my watch. It was twelve noon. I had six more miles to go. I had walked eleven miles in three hours. If I hadn't been loaded and the turnpike hadn't been ice-coated, I could have walked faster. This was slow time. I took a sandwich from my coat pocket Mom had made me bring along. I was surprised to find it frozen. But I was hungrier than I thought. The frozen sandwich tasted good. I ate it as I walked on the Laurel Ridge Road. If ever in my life I had felt a velocity of frigid wind, it was on this road. It went through my overcoat and through my clothes. I thought the terrific force of this wind would lift me from the road over into the Tiber Valley.

I felt the cold as I had never felt it before. My hands and feet ached. Water ran from my eyes. Before I had walked three miles along Laurel Ridge, I would get behind a big tree here and there to serve as a windbreak so I could warm. Often I stood behind a rock cliff for a windbreak. The cold was doing something to my body and my senses. Friday night's sleeping in a fodder shock was warm in comparison. Finally I reached the path where I left the ridge. I was almost too stiff to bend over to get between the fence wires. I wondered if I could go on to Baylors'. Once, I sat down on the snow. I thought of leaving my suitcase and trying to run to warm my body.

As I walked and ran slowly down the mountain, stepping in my own dim footprints I had made Friday, my senses came to me enough to make me realize I had to go on. I couldn't stop now. If I did, I'd soon be a goner. The thought of sitting down again scared me. I hadn't any feeling in my feet. I felt as if I was stepping with wooden feet. My numb, lifeless hand felt chained to my suitcase. I reached Baylors' at two-thirty. It had taken me two and a half hours to cover the last six miles. If it hadn't been for Ottis Baylor, I believe to this day my hands and feet would have been frozen. The first thing he did was take the suitcase from my hand, and then he pulled off my gloves and shoes. I couldn't.

He poured ice-cold water into a tub and had me put my feet in the water. I couldn't feel the water with my feet. He had me put my hands in a pan of ice-cold water. I couldn't feel the water with my hands. In a few minutes Lucretia brought hot water and Ottis tempered the water gradually until a little feeling came back to my hands and feet. He tempered the water more and more. And more feeling came to my hands and feet. He continued this process until the water was approximately body temperature. The normal feeling to my hands and feet was restored.

"I don't know why you had to go to Landsburgh on a day like last Friday," Ottis Baylor said, when I started putting on my socks. "Then you come back here on the coldest day I have ever seen in my life. I wouldn't have slept out on a night like last Friday night, when it was twelve below in the valley; nor have walked back here from Landsburgh on a day like this, for this farm! Why did you do it?"

"Then you know about my getting lost last Friday," I said.

"Everybody knows about it around Winston," he answered. "Everybody's talking about it. Not anybody can understand why you did it," he added thoughtfully, as I slipped my feet back into my shoes.

"You must have a girl in Landsburgh," Lucretia laughed.

"Here is why I did it," I said, as I opened my suitcase. "I'll show you! See these books! I went after these for your boys and for the pupils in my high school. Smartest pupils I've ever taught."

Then Ottis looked at Lucretia, and Lucretia looked at Ottis.

"I did something else, too, you'll hear about in a month from now," I added. "I went to see Superintendent Anderson about a little matter."

"You're not resigning from Winston High School, are you?" Ottis asked.

"Oh, no," I answered. "I wouldn't think of it."

When I told my pupils about a scholastic contest with Landsburgh High School, I watched their expressions. They were willing and ready for the challenge. The competitive spirit was in them.

"We must review everything we have covered in our textbooks," I told them. "We must cover more territory in our textbooks too. Hold up your right hands if you are willing!"

Every pupil raised his hand.

Right then we started to work. In addition to regular assignments, my pupils began reviewing all of the old assignments we had covered.

Despite the challenge ahead and all the reviewing and study we planned to do, we never stopped play. The Tiber River was frozen over. The ring of skates and merry laughter broke the stillness of the winter nights. We skated on the white winding ribbon of ice beneath the high, cold winter moon. Often we'd skate until midnight. We'd hear the wind blow mournfully over the great white silence that surrounded us and sing lonesome songs without words in the barren branches of the bankside trees. And we'd hear the foxes' barking, high upon the walls of sheltering cliffs, mocking the music of our ringing skates.

Over the week ends we'd go to Tiber where we'd cut holes in the ice and gig fish. The boys and I would rabbit-hunt up and down the Tiber Valley in the old stubble fields now covered with snow and swept by wind. We'd track minks, possums, raccoons, weasels, and foxes to their dens. We'd climb the mountains and get spills over the rocks into the deep snow. This took our minds from books and taught us another kind of education. It was as much fun as reading books. Now that a big contest was before us, we needed diversion. And we got it. Our state was not usually cold enough for winter sports. This winter was an exception, and we took full advantage of it.

When we hunted the girls didn't go with us, but when we skated, fished, and rode sleighs they went along. There was a long gentle slope not far from the schoolhouse, we found ideal for our sleighs. It was almost a mile to the end of our sleigh run. We went over the riverbank and downstream for many yards on the Tiber ice. We rode sleighs during the noon hour, before and after school.

On winter days when the snow had melted, leaving the dark earth a sea of sloppy mud, we designed floor games for our little one-room school. They were simple games such as throwing bolts in small boxes. And we played darts. We also played a game called "fox and goose." We made our fox-and-goose boards and we played with white, yellow, and red grains of corn. We had to make our own recreation. I never saw a distracted look on a pupil's face. I never heard one complain that the short, dark winter days were boresome because there wasn't anything to do. I think each pupil silently prayed for the days to be longer. We were a united little group. We were small but we were powerful. We played hard, and we studied hard. We studied and played while the December days passed.

That day in early January, we dismissed school. This was the first time we had dismissed for anything. We had never lost an hour. I had actually taught more hours than was required. This was the big day for us. It was too bad that another blizzard had swept our rugged land and that a stinging wind was smiting the valleys and the hills. But this didn't stop the boys and me from going. Leona Maddox, my best Latin pupil, couldn't go along. Her father, Alex Maddox, wouldn't let her ride a mule seventeen miles to Landsburgh to compete in a contest on a day like this. I couldn't persuade him to let her go.

On that cold blizzardy morning, Budge Waters rode his mule to school very early and built a fire in the potbellied stove. When the rest of us arrived on our mules at approximately seven o'clock, Budge had the schoolroom warm. We tied our mules to the fence, stood before the fire, and warmed ourselves before we started on our journey. Then we unhitched our mules from the fence and climbed into the saddles. Little clouds of frozen snow in powdery puffs arose from the mules' hoofs as six pupils and their teacher rode down the road.

Though the force of wind in the Tiber Valley was powerful, it was at our backs. The wind was strong enough to give our mules more momentum. We made good time until we left the valley and climbed the big hill. Here, we faced the wind. It was a whipping wind—stinging, biting wind on this mountain—that made the water run from our eyes and our mules' eyes, but for us there was no turning back. We were going to Landsburgh High School. That was that. We were determined to meet this big school; big to us, for they outnumbered us twenty-six to one. Soon we were down in Hinton Valley. Then we rode to the top of the Raccoon Hill, where we faced the stinging wind again.

"Mr. Stuart, I have been thinking," Budge Waters said, as we rode along together, "if you can sleep in a fodder shock when it's twelve degrees below zero, we can take this contest from Landsburgh High School! I've not forgotten how you walked seventeen miles to carry us books. All of your pupils remember. We'll never let you down!"

Budge Waters thought of this because we were riding down the mountain where I had slept that night. Then we rode down into the Raccoon Valley, and Billie Leonard, only thirteen years old, complained of numbness in his hands, feet, and lips. He said he felt as if he was going to sleep. I knew what he was talking about. I had had the same feeling the day Ottis Baylor had put my hands and feet in cold water. We stopped at a home, tied our mules to the fence, and went in and asked to warm. Bert Patton, a stranger to us, piled more wood on the open fire until we were as warm as when we had left the schoolhouse. We told him who we were and where we were going.

"On a day like this!" he said, shaking his head sadly.

We climbed into the saddles again. We were over halfway now. The second hitch would put us at Landsburgh High School. We had valley all the way to Landsburgh, with walls of rugged hills on each side for windbreaks.

At eleven o'clock we rode across the Landsburgh High School yard, and hitched our mules to the fence around the athletic field. There were faces against the windowpanes watching us. Then we walked inside the high school, where Principal Ernest Charters met and welcomed us. He told us that he was surprised we had come on a day like this and that we had been able to arrive so soon.

In the Principal's office my pupils and I huddled around the gas stove while we heard much laughter in the high-school corridors. The Landsburgh High School pupils thought we were a strange-looking lot. Many came inside their Principal's office to take a look at us. We were regarded with curiosity, strangeness, and wonder. Never before had these pupils seen seven mules hitched to their schoolyard fence. Never before had they competed scholastically with so few in number—competitors who had reached them by muleback. The Landsburgh High School Principal didn't feel about the contest the way we felt. To him, this was just a "setup" to test his pupils for the district contest which would soon be held. He told me this when he went after the sealed envelopes that held the questions. We warmed before the gas stove while he made arrangements for the contest.

"These questions were made out by the state department of education," he said when he returned. "I don't know how hard they are."

My pupils stood silently by the stove and looked at each other. We were asked to go to one of the largest classrooms. A Landsburgh High School teacher had charge of giving the tests. When the Landsburgh High School pupils came through the door to compete against my pupils, we knew why Principal Charters had selected this large classroom. My pupils looked at each other, then at their competitors.

I entered redheaded Jesse Jarvis to compete with ten of their plane-geometry pupils. I entered Billie Leonard against twenty-one of their selected algebra pupils.

"Budge, you'll have to represent us in grammar, English literature, and history," I said. "And I believe I'll put you in civil government. Is that all right?"

"Yes," he agreed. Budge had never had a course in civil government. All he knew about it was what he had read in connection with history.

"Robert Batson, you enter in history and grammar.

"Robin Baylor, you enter in algebra.

"Snookie Baylor, you enter in algebra and plane geometry.

"Sorry, Mr. Charters," I said, "we don't have anyone to enter in Latin. My best pupil, Leona Maddox, couldn't make this trip."

After the contest had begun, I left the room. Miss Bertha Madden was in charge. I took our mules to Walter Scott's barn on the east end of Landsburgh, where I fed and watered them.

With the exception of an interval when the contestants ate a quick lunch, the contest lasted until 2:30 P.M. I had one pupil, Budge Waters, in four contests. I had planned to enter him in two. Just as soon as Budge had finished with civil government, we started grading the papers. All the pupils were requested to leave the room.

We graded the papers with keys. Mr. Charters, Miss Madden, and two other teachers, and I did the grading. Mr. Charters read the answers on the keys, and we checked the answers. Once or twice we stopped long enough to discuss what stiff questions these were. We wondered how far we would have gotten if we— all of us, college graduates—had taken the same test. One of the teachers asked me, while we graded these papers, if Budge Waters had ever seen these questions before.

When we were through grading the papers, Mr. Charters called the contestants into the classroom.

"I want to read you the scores of this contest," Principal Charters said. His voice was nervous.

"Budge Waters, winner in English literature.

"Budge Waters, winner in grammar.

"Budge Waters, winner in history with almost a perfect score.

"Budge Waters, winner in civil government.

"Why didn't you bring just this one boy?" Principal Charters asked me.

"Because I've got other good pupils," I quickly retorted.

"Billie Leonard, winner in algebra, with plenty of points to spare.

"Jesse Jarvis, second in plane geometry, lost by one point.

"Snookie Baylor and Robin Baylor tied for second place in algebra.

"Congratulations," said Principal Charters, "to your pupils and to you, on your success. It looks as though Winston High will represent this county in the district scholastic contest. I've never heard of such a remarkable thing."

When we left the Landsburgh High School we heard defeated pupils crying because "a little mudhole in the road like Winston beat us."

In a few minutes our mule cavalcade passed the Landsburgh High School. Faces were against the windowpanes and many pupils waved jubilantly to us as we rode by, our coattails riding the wind behind our saddles, and the ends of our scarfs bright banners on the wind.

We rode victoriously down the main street of Landsburgh on our way home.

The news of our victory over Landsburgh High School spread like wildfire in dry autumn leaves. It was talked about in every home up and down the Tiber Valley. Alex Maddox told his neighbors he regretted now he hadn't let Leona go with us. The victory of our little school over Landsburgh High School was not only talked about up and down the Tiber Valley, but the length and breadth of Greenwood County. Superintendent Anderson told his rural teachers, and the rural teachers told their pupils, and their pupils told their parents; and in this way the news reached the entire county. Everybody was proud of us because we were the smallest of the rural high schools and the only one that had ever thought to challenge the scholastic standing of the large Landsburgh High School.

Soon we gave our Superintendent Anderson, his rural teachers, and the people of Greenwood County additional pleasant news. Billie Leonard and Budge Waters entered the district scholastic contest. Budge Waters won three contests: grammar, history, and civil government. Billie Leonard won first place in algebra. Then Billie Leonard took pneumonia fever and couldn't go to the state contest. Budge Waters went alone and captured two first places: history and grammar. I knew my judgment of my pupils wasn't wrong.

I thought about the normal curve system! I was convinced a good teacher recognized ability of his pupils without the help of cataloguing their grades by some theory.

I had to whip Guy Hawkins to give me a reputation in Lonesome Valley. That was the greatest thing I had done in a community where might made right. In Tiber Valley, my pupils had to win scholastic contests. That was the difference. Now I had a reputation as a teacher in Tiber Valley.

Spring brought a new life to all of us. We went back to the field to play ball. We played ball while the girls played croquet. Then we went to the river and dropped our nets. We set our trotlines. It was great fun to get back to the Tiber in the spring. This clear blue water from the limestone country was beautiful, flowing under the fronds of the large willows. Like the Tiber River people, I had come to know this river and to love it. I even tried to write poems about it. This river whose lullabies of rippling waters sang me to sleep every night. . . . This river where I had fished, hunted, and skated; where I had walked in the autumn and had seen the golden leaves float like so many ships sailing to a far-off destiny beyond this valley and these hills. . . . The banks of this river where the trees first leafed and bloomed in spring, I had learned to love. It had become a part of me.

Our school year was coming to a close. We had covered the entire contents of each textbook. We had started over these books again, for the last review. I did not have a pupil fail a course. I had two pupils make average grades. The other twelve ranged from good to superior. The only B's Budge Waters made in his life in school were two in algebra. I had never had a discipline problem.

Pupils had gotten along better than if they had been brothers and sisters. They respected me as much as if I had been their father. I had taught them, had hunted and fished with them. I had accepted and loved the recreation they had made for themselves and for me. I had been one of them even though I was their teacher.

One day after school while I sat on the bank of the Tiber fishing, I heard the green sycamore leaves swish behind me. I was getting a bite on my hook when it happened, but the fish suddenly stopped biting. He must have heard the noise too. A big man wearing a gray suit, cap, white shirt, and bow tie came through the brush.

"Here I find this great teacher fishing!" he laughed. "I'd like to be doing the same thing this time a year, but business," he sighed, "keeps me tied down. I'm Larry Kenwood," he introduced himself, gripping my hand. "I'm Chairman of the Landsburgh City School Board."

"I'm glad to know you," I said.

"Well, to come to the point," he said, "the Landsburgh City Board members have decided to hire you for Principal of Landsburgh High School for this coming school year. It's a big school and your main problem will be discipline, but you have a good reputation and we've decided you're the man. Mr. Charters resigned to take another job."

I was so stunned I couldn't speak for a minute.

"Will you be interested?" he asked.

"Of course," I finally said.

"Then meet with us second Tuesday of next month in the Landsburgh High School office," he said.

"I'll be there," I said.

And the Chairman of the Landsburgh City School Board was off as suddenly as he had come.

After he had disappeared beyond the cloud of tender sycamore leaves, it was hard for me to believe he had approached me to take this big position. It was big to me. Only five years ago I had graduated from Landsburgh High School. I had entered Landsburgh High School by taking an examination. I has passed the examination, making an average of seventy-eight, after having an approximate thirty months of rural school training. I had been perhaps the poorest-trained pupil ever to enter the high school. And now I had been invited back to become Principal. I had been called "polecat" at high school because I had hunted in the autumn and was scarcely ever without a little of the scent. I won't be called "polecat" now! I thought, as I caught the fish that had been biting before Mr. Kenwood had come. Nine years from the time I entered, I go back to take over!

Why do they ask me back? I wondered.

Because Winston High School had defeated Landsburgh High School in the scholastic contests. That was the only reason. That was why they had heard of me. That was why they had come for me instead of my going to them. It was the reputation of my pupils that had brought me this unexpected advancement. It wasn't that I was a good teacher. I had good timber to work with. I had taught the ambitious descendants of a landlocked people, who for the first time in their lives had the advantage of high-school training. They had made the best of it. They had repaid me for everything I had done for them. They had given me their best. I had given them my best. They would return soon to their plowing and planting, to their work beneath the sun, wind, and stars in their valley of mists and tender voices of spring. And I would return to college to take courses in education, to prepare myself for the greater school task ahead.

To Teach, To Love

TO TEACH, TO LOVE was criticized for being disjointed when it appeared in 1970. Like *God's Oddling*, it lacked originality in the sense that it was a bringing together of materials previously published, but those who criticized often overlooked the writer's intent. Like *Mr. Gallion's School*, *To Teach, To Love* belongs to the decade of the sixties, a turbulent decade in which America was undergoing a cultural revolution that would affect our nation's schools profoundly. That it came at the end of the sixties was no accident. (Stuart received the first advance copy in November of 1969.) As early as when he toured Europe on a Guggenheim Fellowship in 1937, Stuart was comparing the American and European systems of education. In 1960-61, however, he lived in Cairo, Egypt, where he taught at American University. In Egypt, he learned the ways of education under an oppressive dictatorship, and the Egyptian experience haunted him throughout the sixties. Apprehensive about the future of America and American education, Stuart never tired of saying that a country can be no better than its schools.

In the last chapter of *To Teach, To Love*, the writer summarizes his teaching career: "As a teacher, I have tried to go beyond the textbooks into the character—stressing honesty, goodness, and making each life count for something. . . . Yes, I have tried to follow my dream—and it has led me to dedicate much of my life to an effort to be an awakening teacher, one like so many of those I knew in my youth, like so many of those who taught me and, later, studied under me." Viewed in its historical context, *To Teach, To Love* ceases to be merely a reshaping of old materials. It is an attempt to create a narrative that will inspire by example and through doing so bring about change. Stuart never lets the reader forget that the challenge to our system of education is one of both literacy and morality. Further, he never lets the reader forget that the future of our civilization depends upon meeting this challenge.

Chapters 1 through 5 of *To Teach, To Love* constitute a narrative of Stuart's preschool and school education except for the summers he spent at George Peabody College. In chapters 6 through 10, however, the emphasis shifts. In the last half of *To Teach, To Love*, Stuart is both working out and articulating a philosophy of education. While formulating his philosophy, he is testing it against practical experience. He knows that a philosophy of education divorced from practice is useless. At least such is the case in *To Teach, To Love*, where philosophy of education is never allowed to dwindle into mechanical manipulation of abstract ideas.

Disjointed or not, reviewers found good things to say about the book in 1970. For example, Jack Anderson described it as a lovely but almost archaic book which "reminds us that our ancestors are still here and their values still true" (*Pasadena Star-News*, 22 February 1970), and Roger D. Bonham saw it as "an expression of powerful beliefs" (*Columbus Evening Dispatch*, 8 February 1970). Winifred R. Gauvreau saw it as a statement of faith in America and American education (*Nevada State Journal*, 15 February 1970); Mary C. Griffith praised Stuart's high regard for American education (*Pensacola News-Journal*, 19 April 1970); Dorothy Hamill noted Stuart's evaluations of his old teachers (*Johnson City [Tennessee] Press-Chronicle*, 21 June 1970); and Ellen Roy Jolly was impressed by Stuart's faith in young people as well as his Jeffersonian faith in the masses (*Baton Rouge Morning Advocate*, 15 March 1970). I saw in *To Teach, To Love* many of the principles of humanism Faulkner borrowed from the ancient Romans (*Laurel Review*, Spring 1970), and Sara S. Nolan saw it as evidence that Stuart was the closest thing to a poet laureate teachers had (*Tennessee Teacher*, February 1970). Finally, Lee Pennington called it a major statement on education and praised Stuart for making such a statement (*Register of the Kentucky Historical Society*, July 1970).

Whether *To Teach, To Love* is a major statement on education or not likely depends on the orientation of the reader. On the other hand, that it was reissued by the Jesse Stuart Foundation in 1987 indicates that someone still thinks it has value, and during this time of crisis in American education it may prove more valuable than reviewers imagined in 1970. In any event, the selection included here contains a number of philosophical statements on education, but, more important, it contains an episode on Stuart as teacher—explaining how he went about teaching students to write.

After teaching in rural schools, after being a high-school teacher and superintendent of Greenup County schools, I knew I needed more know-how to meet the educational problems of my day and time. I decided to study at George Peabody College for teachers, Nashville, Tennessee. Here I spent four summers, equivalent to one year of graduate work. Had I written a thesis, which I never did, I would have received an M.A. degree there. But at Peabody, where graduate students outnumbered undergraduates, I got more than a sheepskin.

Although I didn't realize it at the time, my teachers at Peabody College were educational giants. One of the most outstanding was Dr. Alfred Leland Crabb. I had philosophy of education under this remarkable teacher-writer-lecturer. He asked our class of graduate students to write a paper on our philosophy of life—I thought this over while sitting in class. I came to the conclusion my philosophy (being one of the younger ones in the class) was not solidified enough—that I couldn't write my philosophy yet. I thought I should write on the philosophy of an older person. And who would I choose? I decided before the class was over.

After the bell ending the class, I went up to Dr. Crabb's desk.

"I don't have a philosophy of education," I told Dr. Crabb. "I feel that I can't do your assignment. But I have a substitute if you'll let me do it."

"What is your substitute?" he asked sternly.

"I'd like to write on the philosophy of my Uncle Martin Hilton," I said. "He's my mother's brother, a very positive man. He certainly has a philosophy of life!"

"Is he a teacher?" Dr. Crabb asked.

"No, he's only an eighth-grade graduate," I said. "And he is a Kentucky mountain hillside farmer. And he sat in the shade reading *The Rise and Fall of the Roman Empire* while weeds took his corn!"

"Sounds like a very interesting man," Dr. Crabb said. "I'll let you take your uncle for your philosophy-of-education paper."

On the date Dr. Crabb had wanted our papers, everyone had

his paper ready. At our next class meeting, Dr. Crabb announced: "Today I am going to read the philosophy-of-education paper which I think is best. It is titled 'Uncle Mel,' and was written by Jesse Stuart." I had been an unknown in this philosophy-of-education class up until now. I had asked a lot of questions. Dr. Crabb read my paper while the old graduate students, many of them Ph.D. candidates, listened. This paper created quite a stir. I remember one woman who was working on her Ph.D. said it was more like a short story than a paper on the philosophy of education. One person wiped away a few tears. He said my uncle reminded him of one he had, but he had never thought of him as subject for a term paper.

This time Dr. Crabb asked me to stay after class. He said he wanted to talk to me about my paper. And I waited until all members of the class had left the room.

"Stuart, I've been at Peabody a long time," he said. "Each summer and each year I have my students taking philosophy of education do this paper. This is the best one I have ever received and. . . ."

"Well, thank you, Dr. Crabb," I interrupted him. I was really pleased to have this compliment from him.

"And I think you might sell this paper to a magazine," he said.

"Which magazine would you suggest, Dr. Crabb?" I asked.

"Any of the quality magazines," he replied.

After talking to him, I hurried to my room, put the manuscript in an envelope with a self-addressed and stamped envelope for its return if it were rejected. I sent it to *Esquire*.

That summer I had brought my brother, James, with me to Peabody. We had to live on half enough money to support one of us. I had been teaching for a small wage, and James had been working on my father's farm. We came thinking we could get part-time employment. Some days we didn't know where our food would come from. There was a small restaurant where I could put a nickel in a machine and pull the lever. If the right combination of numbers came up, I was paid off in meal tickets. And I had always been lucky. Once for a nickel I got thirty meal tickets.

"Uncle Mel" had been gone just over a week when my self-addressed envelope, almost flat as a pancake, was returned to me. I tore it open. And here was a fat check—just as if they knew my predicament. But they certainly didn't know I had a brother with me whom I was trying to support!

"Hurrah, hurrah," went through my head as I waved the check. I wanted to celebrate. I ran to Shorty's Restaurant, where I had won so many free meals for us. I bought a cigar! Then I went up the street of the Quadrangle to the administration building. I knew Dr. Crabb would be in his office at this hour. And he would rejoice when I showed him my check.

Inside the administration building I hurried to his office. Up I went, waving the check and puffing my cigar. "Dr. Crabb," I said in a half-breath. "It sold! Look at this!"

"You get out of here!" he yelled. He grabbed a large book. "Get out of here with that cigar!"

When he came after me with a book, I started running. I could have pushed my excellent professor aside easily. He was three-fourths my size and twenty-six years my senior. But I ran like a chicken out of the administration building, down the steps, and down the street. Dr. Crabb followed me to the steps. But I was off and gone.

I had forgotten Dr. Crabb's hatred of tobacco. No one could smoke in his house. A classmate of mine who got his Ph.D. degree at Peabody lighted up a cigar while he waited to form a line in the graduation processional. Dr. Crabb came up and pointed a finger. "If I had known you would have done this, you wouldn't be wearing that cap and gown this evening," he told him. He meant it too.

After selling this paper to *Esquire*, where it was published as a story, I sent more poems, articles and stories to magazines. Things changed for James and me at Peabody College. We ended up eating in the Peabody College cafeteria. I no longer gambled for food. I paid James's and my way in full, and when James and I went home, we didn't go back the way we had come. We went first class on the Pan American—a great southern train. We ate steaks in the diner too. And the money I had sent home to help my father on our farm was enough to purchase some new mule-and-horse-drawn equipment, a new hay rake, a new mowing machine, a new disk, new plows, and a lime spreader. This was one of the most profitable summers I ever spent in college—thanks to Dr. Crabb.

The following summer, when I returned to Peabody to further

my teacher education, new plants came up in Dr. Crabb's garden. He didn't know exactly what they were. He hoed the plants and coddled them. They grew up, beautiful plants with large leaves that flapped in the wind. Beautiful small blue blossoms appeared in the cone at the top of the stem. Dr. Crabb didn't know he was hoeing and loving tobacco plants—something I had worked with many years of my life. It was the money crop on our Kentucky farm. Dr. Crabb, so I learned later, was furious over his mistake. And he never learned who planted those seeds in his garden. Dr. Crabb, giant educator that he was, thought tobacco plants were flowers.

Dr. Crabb suggested that I apply for a Guggenheim Fellowship. I applied and got it. I applied for and got a leave of absence from McKell High School. I went to Europe, where I visited twenty-seven countries; I visited schools in those countries; I visited farms.

"Why don't you go to America, James?" I asked a Scotch friend of mine while I was in Scotland. He was a talented architect and painter and was making seventy-two dollars a month. "You'd make money in America with your talent."

Since I had told him my salary as a teacher in Kentucky, he smiled at me. "You'd better stay in Scotland and teach school," he said. "We pay our teachers more than you make in Kentucky."

And I found that he was right. Though the wages in industry were frightfully low in Scotland (the land of my father's people) as compared to those in America, teachers were better paid. The reason teachers were well paid, so I was informed by knowledge-able sources, was that it took years to prepare a teacher—and it was expensive—whereas a skilled tradesman could learn his trade in a short time and was usually paid something while he was learning.

The teachers I talked with in Edinburgh were earning well over the two-thousand-dollar mark. I did not tell the Scots that I remembered the time when good teachers, well prepared to teach, left the rural schools in Greenup County, Kentucky, be-cause they couldn't live on their low salaries, and sought employ-ment in the five-and-ten-cent stores in Ohio.

However, I didn't fail to tell school administrators and teachers everywhere I visited in Europe that our forefathers had planned a more democratic school system than I had found in any country in Europe. Free high schools did not exist in any country I visited. In England, Scotland, Wales, and Ireland, they had free elementary schools which corresponded to our grade schools and probably reached our junior high schools, since algebra, Latin, mechanical drawing, and plane geometry were taught. But the students left school at about fourteen and went to serve an apprenticeship for some trade.

Our American school system has less snobbishness than the English, and I say this with all due respect for the fine literature and sense of freedom and respect for laws that these great people have given to the world. In America every boy and girl, regardless of family and money, has a chance. In England a coal miner's son is expected to be a coal miner, though if unusually talented he may not be. It made me glad I was born in America.

I found out that schoolteachers in England are not only well paid in comparison with other professions, but they are respected as they are few places in the world. The English are smart enough to know that the fate of their people is decided in the schoolrooms of England. Adolf Hitler, too, was smart enough to organize the schools the way he wanted them organized; he put teachers who were really teachers (and not Nazi puppets) in concentration camps, so he could proceed to sell his ideas to the German people. We know the results.

I visited schools in Denmark, Norway, Sweden, Finland, Estonia, Latvia, Lithuania, Poland, Holland, Belgium, France, Switzerland, Czechoslovakia. In every country I visited—whether or not the people were poor, and most of them were exceedingly poor by our standards—they paid their teachers well in comparison with the wages paid others. Next to England, Sweden paid its teachers best.

America is my country—and I'm as much a product of America as a stalk of Indian maize corn. Therefore I have a right to criticize and praise. And I say that we certainly departed from what our forefathers established in this country. They would have been shocked to see how, although the schools have had the lion's share in bringing about our country's accomplishments, we have let some of our best teachers depart for vocations where they can make a better living. And who can blame them?

Our federal and state governments have not acted to avert

disaster in the schools. What we did in Kentucky was to lower the standards so that any Tom, Dick, or Harry with a high-school education could get an emergency certificate, though he never had a day's teaching experience.

During the war I met a former student who was working in industry. "I just want to show you something," he said. He took a slip of paper from his pocketbook and handed it to me. It was a statement showing that he had earned $138.52.

"I made that in one week."

"Just $1.48 short of what I make in a month as a teacher," I said.

I had taught him four years in high school. He had finished with barely a C average—just enough to "get by." Yet he was not doing manual labor but had taken a six-week course in blueprinting.

At this time, I had approximately seven years of college and university training and ten years of experience. I had spent thousands of dollars for my training. And as superintendent, I was receiving the best pay in our system—$140 a month!

I cannot understand how this nation can underestimate the worth of its schools, when it was founded on the basis of free schools and free religious worship. I am not proud of the way my native country has treated its teachers.

In Edinburgh, Scotland, I kept getting letters signed "Nancy Astor." I didn't know Nancy Astor. She was asking me to come and visit with her in London. I didn't answer her letters. Finally she wrote me in disgust, "Are you or are you not coming to see me?" I had rented a room from Mrs. Hastings, a kind Scottish woman of about sixty. Since I thought someone I didn't know might be trying to blackmail me, I took Nancy Astor's letters to Mrs. Hastings. She said, "Who are you? Who do I have staying here with me? You are receiving letters from Lady Astor! I am in her party, I work for her. I never got a letter from her in my life!"

When Mrs. Hastings said, "Lady Astor," I knew who was writing to me. Lady Astor was a Langley from Virginia who was related to the Stuarts of Virginia. It was distant, but still kinship. I sat down and wrote her I would be there. After leaving Scotland, I visited Northern and Southern Ireland, revisited Wales before getting to London. Then I went straight to Lord and Lady Astor's. It was the largest house I had ever stayed in. I had Godfried Van Cramm's (the great German tennis player) old room at Lady

Astor's. Several mornings I ate breakfast with Lord and Lady Astor.

"What is it you miss most in England that you are used to in America?" they asked me.

"A good cigar," I said.

"Just a minute," she said. She got up from the table and handed me two large cigars.

"Cigars Mr. Winston Churchill left here," she said. "Try these."

"It's a great cigar, Lady Astor," I said. "But I couldn't afford these."

Once the telephone rang in my room and I answered.

"Sir, this is the ambassador of Belgium calling," said a voice.

"You've got the wrong number," I said and hung up.

Lady Astor took me to the House of Commons. Once I sat six seats from the Queen Mother, King George VI's mother. I never had a better time than at the Astors'. Lady Astor gave me a key to the house, a tiny key that unlocked a big door.

Evenings I joined struggling British, Irish, and Welsh poets who had come to London to make literary careers. They certainly were poor and struggling. I liked them and they liked me. The poet-writers would follow me home after our parties broke up, and they'd watch me unlock the door and go into the Astors' big home. But this wasn't the biggest home. It was at Clivedon on the Thames River. And I went there with Lord and Lady Astor for more parties and a two-day stay. I had never worn a tux, but I dressed in my dark $22.50 suit. I looked all right and I felt at home with some of the guests, especially beautiful Lady Astor, whose sons were older than I—I especially felt at home with her in her home. I spent two wonderful weeks with the Astors and was invited to return if and when I ever revisited England. When I left the Astor home, I went to the Continent for more travel and later left for home in America.

When I returned to Kentucky I found that things had changed in our educational system. A rigged election had changed the school-board members. The new members did not want me back at McKell. I had challenged the liquor dealers and the bootleggers. I had rocked the boat. These new board members did not want me in their system at all. I crossed the river to Ohio, and there I got a fine job teaching remedial English in an excellent high school in Portsmouth.

During my schooldays I came to the conclusion that if I ever taught school I'd teach English differently from any teacher I'd ever had except Mrs. Hatton and Mr. Kroll. They were the best, and it seemed to me they got results. Each taught creative writing one day a week in their English courses. Mrs. Hatton couldn't write a good line of poetry or prose herself, yet she could tell her students how to do it. Mr. Kroll was a novelist. These teachers were opposites but obtained very similar results. I have no way to measure the results of their teaching except by remembering the work that was read in each class.

My early training left me with the idea that writers were not exactly human beings, that they walked, talked, loved, breathed, and ate like the rest of us living mortals here, but yet they were different. They wore long beards and chin whiskers. I wanted to be a writer, but could I ever qualify according to my preconceived image? I wonder if any students today feel like that. Well, if they do, it is nonsense. Writers are real human beings.

When I first meet a new class of English students, I tell them that I don't want them to feel that they aren't a real part of things. I want everybody to feel as welcome as the flowers of May on the big earth. I tell them that I seldom flunk an English student, and this usually pleases the class. It is true an English student has to be downright hopeless before I flunk him. I want my students to have absolute freedom and see what they do with it. That is something I seldom got when I was a student. Teachers sooner or later will find that the students themselves create their own interest. The classwork will become fun, and once there's interest in the classroom, discipline naturally follows.

In order to get things going, I tell the students to write about anything they like and put it in any form they please. The race begins. They envy each other. They try to do better work than their friends, and they jump so far ahead that I find some students start copying. They don't intend to be outdone. I have seen teachers who would throw a student out of the class for a trick like this. But why should the student be thrown out? You understand he has pride, and he hates to let another surpass him when he stands up and reads before the class once a week. It is usually the girls that will not be outdone. The boys can take it better than the girls.

My first aim is to get them to write. I don't grade off for periods and commas and colons and semicolons when I'm getting them interested in putting their thoughts on paper. Remember, there are a few in the class who can't write a line. They are afraid to let themselves slip on paper, as they would be afraid to skate the first time on ice. I take these students one by one, find out an impressive experience they have had, and ask them to write about it. It is not long before they find out they can write themes, poetry, articles, and short stories, in a fashion. I want them to feel free and flexible. I want them to put their hearts on paper, and they do it.

I let the students have memory work once a week, and this is optional too. If it is an American-literature class, I ask them to memorize American poetry; if the class is English literature, I ask them to memorize poetry from the English poets.

Many students ask to memorize more than one selection of poetry. I can hardly think of a good minor poem, English or American, that has not been recited in one of my English classes. The minute a student gives a poor poem for memory work one can see the students looking at each other. They set their own standards of memory work and give as much or as little of it as they like.

Written work grows like memory work. First the themes are brief. Then they get longer and still longer, until they become quite lengthy. We have taken up a whole period on one theme, discussed it pro and con, and each student raises his voice and gives his opinion. We let everybody's point of view count. If a student doesn't fit into our English class, we try to find the reason and to remove all obstacles. We discuss the form of the poetry when it is recited. We try to forget that the author was a literary figure. We find lines in his poetry that show he was a real human being like the rest of us. Then, when we study his life, we hunt for poems that relate to incidents of his time. It makes the English class fun.

I read poems from my own book to my English classes, and I often find one or two of the students start to imitate my work. I read stories to them and articles. I find that my classes are critical, and when the majority say a poem is good, or a story, it sooner or later finds a place in print. This has happened too many times to be an accident. I've been thoroughly disgusted at times, when they'd turn their thumbs down on my work. But they stuck to their judgment, and they were usually right.

All members of the class agree at the first of the year to write about the things in our own backyards. We would write about anything and everything except picnics (that was a subject worn out long ago) and trips to New York, unless the student had actually been there. We decided to write about our own people, our trees, stars, grass, flowers—old apple orchards in the sun and tumbling fences, people getting drunk, elections, public officials, love affairs that the students actually know of (one of their own if they want to write it), snakes, turtles, terrapins, birds—all living things that walk or crawl on the earth. There is no barrier to keep them from writing about anything. Length and style are left to them. Outside students want to leave their classes and come in and listen to the students read on theme days. Often a student reads a theme and another says, "Why in the world didn't I think about that and write it?" Here it is—just as simple as falling off a log, and someone happened to stumble onto the idea and put it into words. That is the way great art is born—it is often done when the author doesn't realize what he is doing.

One year I couldn't get any poetry from the class. This was back at McKell. The students wanted to write prose. I asked for poetry time and again. It never came. One day a student from our little Writers' Club (which at that time was composed of five boy members) handed me five poems. I handed them back and asked Clyde to read them aloud. I asked him if he had ever written poetry before, and he said he had, but he had never brought it to class. I thought it was the best poetry I'd ever received from a high-school student. He had scribbled these five poems down in a chemistry class on the backs of his test-question sheets.

I had to suspend another one of my best creative English students twice and threaten to keep him out indefinitely for drinking. He was tall, high-strung, and extremely nervous. The boy could actually write, and he had a mountain of an urge in him to write. He would sit in another class, answer the questions thrust at him by the teacher, and in the meantime be writing a short story. He told me many times that he would rather write than eat. I would not change his style of writing for anything on earth. He was a little rough, but sooner or later as he grew older he would make the necessary changes and shape himself up into a regular style.

One of the girls wouldn't read a theme in class. One of the teachers told me, "Virginia is afraid of you."

I said in astonishment, "That certainly is strange. She has no right to be afraid of me. No human being needs to be afraid of me. Why, animals are never afraid of me."

"Yes, but Virginia is," she said.

One day I asked Virginia to remain after class. She told me she couldn't talk as she'd like to talk, and when I called on her to read, it scared her. And she thought she couldn't write. I asked her if she could not talk a little. She acknowledged that she could. "Write just as you talk," I told her. The next day she came to English class with a short story. From that time on, she led that English class, with plenty of points to spare. I never found a better all-around English student than Virginia. One day before Virginia graduated, I said to her, "Virginia, see how much a teacher misses when he doesn't understand one of his students. Look at the difference in your work the first semester and the last semester of this year."

Virginia replied, "And how much the student misses when she doesn't understand the teacher! I don't even know what my grades have been this last semester, I've enjoyed my class so much. I've really learned how to express myself on paper, though I do not intend ever to be a writer."

Before the year is over we cut the production down to a certain extent and do a little work on sentence structure. We practice a little technique. At the first of the year, ideas for writing are the things we fight for. Now it is our work to arrange them properly. I have always felt that if the young plastic mind of the student is taught to create—or rather, is directed in its own creation—that the technique would take care of itself. Almost anyone can get to the place where he can punctuate, but can he put his ideas on paper? My feeling is that they cannot when they are hampered by restrictions such as assigned topics to write about, and arguing all day about where a period or comma should be placed. They cannot get anywhere.

I have received letters from English teachers asking me how I teach the short story to high-school English students. These teachers seem to think I should be a better teacher of the short story than those who have never written a story. If anything, this theory should be reversed. The teacher who has never written a short story will not lean to any particular type but will teach each type, written by many different authors, with the same interest.

One thing I do is not to teach the short story as it was taught to me. I used to dread coming to a short story in my literature book. I didn't know anything about the short story; yet I had to dissect it. I had to find the climax, the anticlimax, and about a half-dozen other things in the teacher's formula—a formula creaking with age. I received low marks on dissecting the short story. I graduated from high school hating the short story.

My students, no matter how poor they are, will not leave my English class hating the short story as a medium of literary expression. I shudder at the thought of the English teachers who have ruined their students' love of the short story by age-old tomfoolery. I want my students to enjoy the short story, and they do.

In my assignment of a short story in the text, I ask my students to read the story before we get to class. There will be a few students who have not done this. I make allowances for them. Paragraph by paragraph, we read the story in class. There isn't any hurry with this first short story. Many of the students will not like this story, and they are free to tell me their opinions—maybe they are right. I tell them there are many stories that I do not like, but we go on. We read the story; then we discuss the author, the type of man he was, and why he would write a short story of this type. We also connect the setting and characters with the author. We talk about the words he has used. We discuss this story in general. We do not have a skeleton to analyze the story by; we do not take it apart and piece it together again.

After we have read a few stories in our textbook, we make comparisons of the short stories of certain authors, for instance, Edgar Allan Poe and Washington Irving. We find that each was a great short-story writer, that Poe depicted the very essence of gloom in his stories, while Irving had a great sense of humor. We do not say one is greater than the other; each student takes his choice. My students often tell me the reason Poe was so morbid in his writing was that he did too much drinking. I tell them that he couldn't have done all the drinking credited to him, since when he died at forty he had written forty-two books. Then we discuss

Poe the entire period. Our class is not on schedule; we never finish a lesson in our allotted time.

You would be surprised what these discussions do. They motivate my students to find out all they can about Poe and bring their information to the next English class. They will tell me that I am wrong about this or that. I listen to the student, often agreeing with him, for I know that I have him where I want him when I get him interested. Interest will bring about love for any subject. Lazy boys get interested in my classes. All of my students get interested. They do not take the textbook for everything. They go to the library of their own accord and look up material.

I tell my students that America is the home of the short story. We go back to the beginning of our literature in America and go over the early giants. We link the writers together, one after another, up to the present time. We discuss the short story from Irving and Poe to Bill Saroyan. I know Bill personally and I tell them about him and many other American authors whose work they study. I try to get the idea out of their heads that all writers wear long beards, that there is something different about them. I tell them authors are human as students are and that someday one in my class may become a fine writer and that he may be a student to whom I have given low marks.

We do not read a short story with sober faces. We relax and take it easy. I want students to laugh in my class when they find something funny in a short story. And if one finds something that would cause him to weep in my class, I would want him to weep. I like most to hear rich laughter in my classes. We read the short stories for enjoyment and with this enjoyment comes knowledge.

We sum up our adventures at the end of the school year in our reading of the various short stories. We note the different periods of American literature, the airtight plot of an O. Henry short story. Many of the modern stories have, as we term it, a subconscious plot. We read the modern story and think it's pointless, but there is some part of it that lodges in one's brain. This type of story, I tell them, is not the planned money-making commercial short story. It is one the author had on his brain and in his heart and had to write. We go in for all these little details in the short story and discuss them with laughter and heated arguments.

My teaching, I'm proud to say, has been felt by college and university English teachers. One lady remarked to me that she was always glad to get my students in her English classes. "They have a broad view and scope of American literature," she said. That was one of the finest compliments that has ever been paid me. I would have felt insulted if she had told me they knew the exact place to put a comma. They have a pretty good knowlege of grammar too, for I lay it on, but the English language, and the great literature that it embraces, is something bigger than mere technicalities. And of all the forms of its literature, the short story is most definitely American.

In my later years of secondary-school work I became weary of tests and testings. And also distrustful. And for very good reasons. My remedial students in that Ohio school have amounted to more in later life than their fellow students classed as excellent. Other pupils in the school used to come to our remedial classes and listen to my pupils read their themes and poetry.

But I am a Kentuckian, not an Ohioan, and after my time in Europe and in Ohio, I wanted to go home. Still our local school system was dominated by politicians who cared more for their power and their jobs than they cared for Kentucky schools. They had no use for me. I bought a farm in W-Hollow next to my father's farm. I married my girl, Naomi Deane, whom I had courted for years and could never marry on the salaries Kentucky paid her teachers. I settled down to farm the land, as my father had before me, and to write. I said that I was through with teaching and schools forever. I have said so time and again, but education is in my blood and bones. I am a schoolman, whether I like it or not. I always come back.

I did write during those first years after my marriage. I wrote poems and short stories and novels. *Beyond Dark Hills,* which I wrote as a term paper for Dr. Mims at Vanderbilt, was published then. It was the first book I had written, but the fourth I had published. *Harvest of Youth, Man with a Bull-Tongue Plow,* and *Head o' W-Hollow* all came into print before it. *Taps for Private Tussie* I wrote in six weeks of hard work at W-Hollow. *Foretaste of Glory* I wrote while serving in the navy during World War II. *The Thread That Runs So True* I wrote and published after the war. Teachers liked this book. The National Education Association voted it the most important book of 1949, and I received many, many invitations from that time onward to address high-school youths and college youths and teachers and principals.

My father, Mitch Stuart, who couldn't read, was a great teacher.

Greenup was the center of my father's universe. He never traveled a fifty-mile radius from this town. He went to town on Saturday, dressed in his overalls, clean blue work shirt, overall jacket, his soiled weathered cap with a shrinking bill, and his turned-at-the-toes, stump-scarred brogan shoes. He walked a path four miles over the bony hills to the town, as he had done since I could remember.

One day I went with him. He talked to a group of men on the courthouse square, where the men from all over the county meet on Saturdays with the men from the town, where they walk, tell their stories, chew their tobacco, try to whittle the longest shavings with their pocketknives while they listen to the courthouse bell calling men inside the courthouse for justice. While they talked and chewed tobacco from long home-grown twists of burley and spit mouthfuls of ambeer spittle on the courthouse square, I heard a man say, who was standing in another group of men not far from my father's group, "There's old overalled Mitch Stuart. . . . See 'im in town every Saturday." This fairly well-dressed man, teacher of a rural school, pointed to my father, and the men in his group looked and listened while he talked. "Never amounted to anything in his life. Never will amount to anything. But he's got smart children. His boy is a book writer, you may've heard about."

Pert Maldin didn't see me as he went on telling the men in his group how my father loved to come to town on Saturdays and loaf, just loaf and try to whittle the longest shavings, how he loved the sound of the courthouse bell and how he'd listened to it for a half-century. And he told them he'd known my father that long and how my father had gone to the same little tavern, run by the same people for a half-century, and got his beer on Saturdays, and after he had a few beers, how he talked to his old friends and told them big windy tales. He told about his seeing my father have a few fights in his younger days and how time had slowed him down. Since Pert Maldin talked confidentially to the men that surrounded him, I couldn't hear all he said. I did hear him say my father wouldn't know his name if he would meet it in the road, that he couldn't read a beer sign, and he couldn't write his name. I thought about walking over and popping Pert Maldin on the nose when he talked about my father. But I stood silently and listened as long as I could, and many thoughts flashed through my brain as the ambeer spittle flashed brown in the November sunlight from the mouths of the men in the group where my father was talking, where they were laughing at some story one of his group had told. I thought a pop on the nose would serve Pert Maldin right, and then I thought, "What's the use? What does he know about my father? And what does he know about education, though he is a schoolteacher?"

My father never read anything about soil conservation in his life. He could not read. I never heard him use the word "conservation." I doubt that he would have known what it meant. It would have been a big word to him. He called it "pertectin' the land." And if anyone had read to him about how to conserve the soil or protect the land, and if he had sat still long enough to listen, I know he would have said: "I did that fifty years ago."

For fifty-five years, ever since I was big enough to tag at his heels, I could vouch for that. He had done everything I've read about soil conservation, and more.

He couldn't understand why everybody didn't "pertect the land." He wondered why more people didn't use a little "horse sense" to keep all their topsoil from washing away.

Despite his not being able to read, in magazines or books, he read the surface of the earth, in every slope, hollow, creek bottom, on every piece of terrain he walked in his day and time. He loved the feel of the soil against his shoe leather and of the fresh dirt in his hand. He almost petted the earth beneath him as if it were something to be fondled and loved.

When he bought the first and only land he ever owned, fifty acres of hill land in the head of W-Hollow, half of this small boundary was considered worthless. He bought the fifty acres for three hundred dollars. The only part of this farm that was not streaked with deep gullies was the timbered hill slopes. The slopes that had been cleared and farmed were streaked with gullies deeper than a man's height. My friends and I used to play on this farm. We cut long poles, and our favorite sport was pole-vaulting from one side of the gully to the other with a sixteen-foot pole. This gives some idea of the ugly scars that marked the earth's surface and gleamed yellow in the sun. Now, no one would know that the skin of this earth had ever been scarred by ugly wounds that cut down deep into the earth's flesh. For this land grows four crops of alfalfa each season, and a mowing machine rolls smoothly over it.

Even when we were cutting logs to build us a home on this farm, he saved the branches and the tops of these trees. The branches from the pine tops especially appealed to him for the kind of soil protection he planned. He laid this brush down in these scars, putting the tips uphill. "When the water comes down the gully," he said, "all the grass, dirt, and little twigs it carries will catch in this brush. The gully will soon fill up." These were deep gullies, and it took wagonloads of brush. We seldom put rocks in one of these gullies. If we did, we put them on the bottom, down deep, so they would never work to the top of the ground and be a menace to the plow or the mowing machine. And we stacked the brush high above the earth's surface in these deep gullies, because the weight of snow, the falling of rain, the wash of sediment weighted it until the brush was finally below the surface. Then we added more brush, finer brush, always placing the tips uphill to meet the avalanche or trickle of water.

My father always said if a cut on the surface of the earth was properly handled, it was like a cut on a man's body, and nature would do wonders to heal it. Nature did wonders where we piled this brush. Nature edged in with her sediment wash. Nature pushed the skin of her surface over, trying to heal the ugly scar. For a year or two or three, we plowed up to these deep gullies. We plowed all around them. The dirt went over and into the brush. Soon we hauled wagons of oak leaves from the woods and spread them over the place where the brush had sunk. We pushed in more dirt from the sides, healing the great scar, and then we started plowing over. We reunited the earth's skin, leaving it without a blemish. It did not take long to do this. My father was always against building rock walls across the gullies. He said it took too long to build the wall, and nature would not work as gently and as fast with rock walls as it would with the brush and the leaves and the pine-needled branches. This was the way he handled the gullies that were from five to fifteen feet deep.

The little gullies, those from six inches to five feet, were much easier to handle. We used what we had cleared from the land to fill them. We pushed the dirt with mattocks and shovels until it united over the brush-brier and leaf-filled gullies. We closed the little scars on the earth's surface before they grew to be big scars. We crossed over the scars with a plow the first year, reuniting what had once been joined. But man's folly had lacerated this earth's surface. Then man had abandoned this land as worthless, never good again for crops, to the wind, rain, and freeze.

"An ounce of prevention is worth a pound of cure," was an old saying my father used when he and I worked on his farm together. Never did I see him one time ever drag a plow up or down a hill and leave a mark that would start a ditch. Maybe that was one of the many reasons why everybody we ever rented from, before he bought land of his own, wanted him to remain on his farm. Instead of dragging a plow with a mule or a mule team hitched to it as I've seen so many other one-horse farmers do in my day, my father would drive his team ahead and carry his plow. He was that careful with other people's land, more careful than the owners themselves, because he loved the land.

Another thing he did from the time I could remember was to follow the contour of the hill with his plow. We never farmed anything but hills in those days and many of them were very steep. These hills didn't erode for my father. He could judge the nature of flowing water, what it would do to the land he plowed. He didn't let it do anything; he never gave it a chance. Even on these hill slopes were deep ravines. My father plowed into them and straight around on the other side, making a perfect contour, never up or down. And he never had a ditch to start down his slope.

Today it is recommended by the Department of Agriculture, and this information is carried to us by our county agent, that we farm corn on our level acres and sow our hill slopes in grass and use the uplands for pasture. My father learned this long ago. Again it was a matter of "horse sense" and he learned, perhaps, the hard way. On our "worthless" (never worthless to us) hillside acres that wouldn't grow timber but only shaggy brush, we cleared this land and farmed it three years straight in corn. We did this to prepare it for grass. We used fertilizer even when we planted the corn with a hand corn-planter. Dad planted the corn, and I followed and dipped fertilizer from a bucket with a spoon. This was before fertilizer became popular in this section. It was before any great farm program was developed. Our first year gave us a fair yield of corn. Our second year the land was easier to plow, since we'd torn out more roots and stumps, and we got a better yield of corn. Then the third year, we got about the same yield as we did the first year.

Then it occurred to my father that this land was already infertile to begin with and that he would not "corn it to death." So my father stopped growing corn on the hillsides altogether. We cut the brush, put it in the ditches if we had them; if we didn't have them, we burned this brush and sowed the land in grass.

We learned the stumps were better left in the ground to rot and fertilize the ground instead of farming the land and tearing out stumps with the plow, digging them up or blowing them out with dynamite. Though we had to cut the sprouts and briers with mattocks and scythes in July and August of each summer, we soon had a better pasture on the steep hills by doing this than we did by raising corn three seasons to prepare the ground for grass. We lifted the fertility of our little creek bottoms, the flats on our hill slopes, and the level hilltops by using oak leaves, barnyard manure, and commercial fertilizer.

We had two places on my father's fifty-acre farm that gave us trouble. One was a steep bluff, not far from the house, that was cleared and farmed. In the first place, this land should have never been cleared. But my father learned this after it was too late. This bluff started slipping off down into the valley in big slides. Again we hauled brush and laid it down in the valley to catch the slides. Then my father did something else. He suggested that we set this slope back in trees. It was a difficult type of erosion, the kind that he thought only the roots of trees would cure. And this would have to be done quickly by trees that had good roots and grew quickly. He decided on the yellow locust sprouts to set on this bluff. Because this tree grew all over the farm, we could find small sprouts to dig and reset. He chose this tree because it had roots like iron ropes, grew rapidly, and made good fence posts when it grew up. He chose it too because the grass would grow under its shade. These locusts stopped the slides on this steep slope. The scars were soon healed, and the land reset itself in grass.

The other problem we had was where a stream sank in our pasture field and left a deep hole. Here is what we did about it. For some time we used this hole for a trash dump. We hauled the old tin cans, trash, cornstalks, and whatnots and dumped them into this hole. But we couldn't fill it up with all of this flimsy material. Then we hauled wagon loads of rocks. They sank down too. Again my father hauled brush and put it into this hole to form some sort of bottom. Then he went about the farm and gathered all the old rolls of barbed wire that we had taken down and rolled up. He hauled these bales of worthless rusty wire, for he was always afraid to leave them about on account of the cattle, mules, or horses, which might get tangled up in them. These he put on top of the brush, and this held the wash that poured into it. The place healed over, and grass covered the spot. No one, except we who remember, because we worked there, would know where it is today. My father worked carefully with nature and she healed her own wounds. Not a scar was left on his eroded fifty acres seven years after he bought the farm.

All his life, he waged his war against erosion. He used a sled to haul tobacco, hay, and fodder down a hill slope. He would not use a wagon because the wagon wheels cut deep and help to start ditches. Sled runners slide over the dirt and hardly leave a trace. He would not drag logs straight down a hill unless the ground was frozen. Old log roads are another good way to start erosion. And if nature, with a bountiful rain, a freeze, or a thaw, broke the skin anywhere, he immediately did something about it before it got a head start. This is why he had no erosion on his farm. He did not learn the second-hand way, through words on a printed page, but he read the language that nature scrawled upon her rugged terrain, and he understood that language better than any other man I have ever known.

Let Pert Maldin talk on the courthouse square. Let him talk about my father's not having an education, that he wouldn't know his name if he'd meet it in the big road. I could tell Pert that he didn't know about education. He was speaking about these sec- ondhand things called books when my father's people had lived an education while they were helping to build a nation and a civilization. Yes, they had taken the law in their own hands, for they had to do it, since the law didn't protect them while they fought their enemies; helped to build the railroads through the mountains and bridges to span the rivers, and blasted the turn- pikes around the rocky slopes. They cleared the fields and broke the first furrows through the roots. They built the log cabins from the giant trees they didn't split into fence rails; they hauled giant saw-logs with yokes of oxen to the edge of the Big Sandy and waited for the spring rains, when with spiked boots and with long poles with spikes in the end they took their log rafts down the Big Sandy and the Ohio River to the little town of Cincinnati, the Queen City of the West.

I could tell Pert Maldin that my father, son of these figures of the earth, with the blood of these men flowing through his veins, was an educated man. He was educated the same as they were educated—but maybe his education didn't fit the time he was living. He couldn't sit behind a desk wearing a white shirt, a necktie, a neatly pressed tailored suit, and shined shoes, with a pencil behind his ear. He couldn't live in a world of figures and words. They would be playthings on the wind to him. All he'd say, even if his mind were trained to do these things, is, "To hell with this." I knew him well enough to know that he would say these words. For what did he say about my books? "A lot of damned foolishness."

I could tell anybody that my father was an educated man. Though he was a small man with a wind-parched face the color of the autumn earth, my father had the toughness in his muscles of the hickory sprout. He had a backbone like a saw-log. In his makeup fear was left out. That word was not in his vocabulary. I never heard him say, in my lifetime, that he was afraid of anything.

My father could take a handful of new-ground dirt in his hand, smell of it, then sift it between his fingers, and tell whether to plant the land in corn, tobacco, cane, or potatoes. He had an intuition that I could not explain. Maybe Pert Maldin, with all his education, could explain it. And my father knew when to plant, how to plant and cultivate, and the right time to reap. He knew the right trees to cut from his timber for wood to burn, and the trees to leave for timber. He knew the names of all the trees, flowers, and plants that grew on his rugged acres. My father was able to live from sterile, rugged mountain soil. He raised enough food for his family to eat, and his family ate about all he raised. Money did not mean food to him, as it does to many in America today. Money was some sort of a luxury to him. It was something he paid his taxes with. Money was something to him to buy land with. And the land and everything thereon was more than a bank account to him; land is something durable, something his eyes could see and his hands could feel. It was not the second-hand substance he would have found in a book.

I could tell anybody in America that if my father wasn't an educated man, we don't have educated men in America. And if his education wasn't one of the best educations a man can have, then I am not writing these words and the rain is not falling today in Kentucky. If his education wasn't as important as mine—this son of his he used to tell every day to go to school, since he had found the kind of education he had didn't work as well this day and time in America as the kind of education where a man had a pencil behind his ears and worked in a world of figures, words, dollars and cents, when to buy, when, where, and how to sell— then I am not writing these words.

"Come with me, Jane," I said. "It's time for your after-school lesson."

Our daughter Jane had come from school and had laid away her books. She was about twelve years old then.

"I'm ready, Daddy," she said.

Jane was always anxious for these little walks we took unless she was reading a book. She was especially ready if her mother had some little task for her to perform. "We're going over on Breadloaf Hill this afternoon," I said.

Jane and I walked in the clean young wind of an afternoon in April. It was about four, and the sky was blue and the sun rather warm. We walked down the W-Branch and Jane left me, ran full speed forward, and leaped into the air, over the stream, and landed on the other side. She was not much given to any athletic performance, and I was very happy to see her do this.

She remained on the other side and watched me walk down to the stream's edge and step gently over and climb the other bank.

Then Jane and I followed a faint path that cattle had made years ago and the elements—rain, freeze, and thaw—had not completely obliterated. There was a dim outline, an indentation in the earth for us to follow. We gradually climbed, following this path that angled up and around the hill, until we came in sight of the first trailing arbutus.

"Oh, Daddy," Jane said. "Here it is! Look! What pretty blossoms! I believe it's prettier than percoon!"

Jane walked up to this beautiful wildflower that grew in a soil almost too poor to grow pines. It was almost too steep to stand on without holding to a bush or tree for support. Below us were the cliffs, and not very deep beneath the surface of this sterile soil was the solid rock. And down below the cliffs was the stream, W-Branch, that carried the bright clean April water from the entire watershed of this valley.

We stood in a beautiful setting with barren trees all around us except for the evergreen pines. At our feet were a few clumps of trailing arbutus, one of our earliest-blooming wildflowers. The small blossoms were shell pink, almost the color of shale stones I'd seen slivered from this hill after a winter freeze. The trailing-arbutus leaves were green and beautiful, just an inch or so above the cold April sod.

"Jane, what kind of leaves remind you of the trailing-arbutus leaves?" I asked her.

"Sand-brier leaves."

"But there's another leaf more like it."

She became studious and thoughtful as we leaned over, touched, and fondled the trailing arbutus.

"Daddy, it must be a sweet-potato leaf," she said. "Trailing arbutus got its name because it grows close to the ground, and sweet potatoes vine over the ground but don't have blossoms."

"Right," I said. "You got that one."

We spent several minutes in this nook of trailing arbutus. And this brought back memories to me. The first time I had ever been on this hill was in the spring of 1915, when my father and mother moved to the house where we live now.

My oldest sister, Sophia, and I were playing on this hill, and we found this flower. We didn't know what it was, and Sophia took a small spray of these exquisite blossoms to the house to show to our mother. Mom told us what they were as soon as she saw them. Since 1915 we have often returned to see trailing arbutus in blossom, to show it to our children and our friends.

It doesn't matter how cold the winter gets, how deep the ground freezes, how poor the soil is, how near the greenbriers and bushes crowd in, the trailing arbutus, so fragile in its beauty, is a rugged little flower, and it holds on to life despite hard winters and rough terrain.

As we sat there, I explained all of this to Jane. And I explained that flowers often remain in the same ground for over a century.

And since our house has stood, with the exception of new additions that we have built, since 1840, I wouldn't doubt that children and adults for 115 years have come each spring to this very same spot to fondle, touch, love, and enjoy the fresh spring beauty this little flower gives. Jane was fascinated with all this.

"The trailing arbutus grows on this bank like our people live in this valley," she said.

"Only the trailing arbutus has been on this bluff longer than we have been in this valley," I said.

Jane looked thoughtfully back at this wistful flower as a cool, brisk April wind whined close against the earth and made its blossoms tremble. We continued our walk up and around the old cattle path.

"What is this?" I asked her, pointing to a tree.

"An oak."

"What kind?"

"I don't know the kind."

"It's a chestnut oak," I told her. "You can tell by the bark. See how big, thick, and tough the bark is."

"How do you know?" she asked me.

"My father and I used to peel chestnut oak for tanbark," I explained. "The bark was used in tanning hides. That means to take the hair off skins, and the skins were made into leather, and the leather into shoes, pocketbooks, saddles, briefcases, suitcases, and a hundred other useful items. This chestnut oak has helped to do all that. Now, will you remember a chestnut oak next time you see one?"

"I believe so!"

"What's this tree?"

"Oh, it's an oak too," she said, smiling. "It's a white oak. I'd know it anyplace by its gray bark."

"You're right. Now, what's that tree?"

"Is it a beech?"

"No, you missed," I replied. "What tree do we get sugar and syrup from? Syrup that's good to eat in the morning with pancakes!"

"It's a sugar maple," she shouted.

"Do you suppose you'll remember this tree when you see it again?" I said. "It does resemble a beech a little, but when both trees leaf, you can tell the difference by their leaves. I want you to be able to tell them apart in the wintertime after they've shed their leaves and they are somber, barren, and sleeping."

"I know what this is before you ask me," Jane said, stopping beside our path to touch a tree. "It's what you make fenceposts of. This is a locust."

"Right this time," I said. "There are two kinds of locust that grow here. This is the black locust."

"How can you tell?"

"By the bark," I told her. "But don't you try to do this yet. Black locust bark is finer than yellow locust bark. I'm going to wait until I've promoted you to a higher grade in this subject I am teaching you, which we call naturelore, before I start giving you the hard problems."

Jane ran and leaped like a spring butterfly flitting from the brisk April wind. She jumped up and down, and the wind lifted her pony tail of brown hair, which was the color of many of the leafless trees that grew in abundance on either side of the dim prints of the path we followed.

We stopped a minute to listen to the singing April wind among these briers and barren trees and to listen to the mumbling April stream, full of clear water, winding down its rockbound channel and singing on its long journey to the sea.

I knew this was a beautiful classroom for my child. It was so large, well ventilated, and decorated with beautiful and wonderful things to inspire a child's thinking.

And I knew similar classrooms existed nearby or not far distant for other children. Many of these classrooms have different decorations from ours, since they're in all parts of America. But parents, teachers, and leaders of youth can take pupils to this kind of classroom everywhere. And I know it gives them a sixth, seventh, and maybe an eighth sense of fundamental knowledge that helps with health and all other subjects, including regular classroom textbooks.

This is an interesting classroom, where, if and when a child finds an interest, there is never any delinquency. And this is the kind of classroom that hurts the trade of the psychologist and the psychiatrist.

Jane started asking her own questions and giving me her answers. This was very good. I knew that in a matter of minutes in nature's big book where there are so many unwritten things to learn, she would trip herself on one of her own questions. Even in this primary course of simple identification, she could not go far.

"Greenwood moss here, and this is mountain tea," she said.

She stopped to pick some leaves to chew, and so did I. And among the mountain-tea stems were ripened red berries that we ate.

"What's this?" I asked.

"I don't know."

"Wild-huckleberry stems."

"And this?"

"It's a maple."

"No, you really missed on that one," I said. "Did you ever see a maple with white blossoms on it? That's a hard one. That's the same tree my father took me to see when I was a small boy. That's a service tree, a serviceberry tree, and many of the older people, including my father, called it a whitebeam tree. I didn't expect you to get that one.

"But remember, it blooms before the dogwood, wild crab apple, and redbud. I've seen it white with blossoms in a March snowstorm, and I couldn't tell its petals and the falling flakes apart.

"It's blooming late this year," I told her. "This has been a late spring. And we've got to get back down home. Look at the sun going over the hill, won't you! Our big classroom will soon be filled with shadows, and the night animals and birds will awake in holes underground, in hollow logs and trees and big nests of leaves up in the vines, and all start stirring in the night world they know. Even the foxes will come from under the cliffs."

"There's a lot to this course," Jane said.

"Sure, there is," I agreed with her. "More than you or I either will ever know."

"But it's fun to learn it, and I feel so good getting out where I can run," she said. "I even like to talk in my classroom."

"Yes, the big hills catch your voice and hold it," I said. "Your voice is lost on the air and mocked by the wind. We are very small in nature's classroom. And so are the ants which we must study at some later date."

We turned on the path and started back down toward the cliffs, stream, the valley, and home. Jane was as happy as I had ever seen any child who had come from a classroom. For the wind among the barren trees was mocking our voices, and the water in the stream below was singing, and the sunball was a red zero of flame.

They were good years and fruitful years, living with Naomi Deane and Jane in W-Hollow, writing and farming and leaving the valley only to go on speaking tours. I wrote *Hie to the Hunters* and *Kentucky Is My Land* and *The Good Spirit of Laurel Ridge*, and in one year I gave eighty-nine talks in thirty-nine states. In 1954 Kentucky made me her poet laureate, and I made more speeches than ever.

In the fall of 1954 I gave a talk at Murray State College. It lasted an hour, and when it was over I was supposed to go and catch an airplane to Flora, Illinois, to give another talk. But I did not take the airplane, and I did not give another talk that day. I fell to the ground with a massive heart attack, and it was a year before I stood on my feet again.

When I was released from the hospital, still a weak man, I went back home to W-Hollow to recover.

Whatever I am or ever shall be—schoolteacher, tiller of the earth, poet, short-story writer, upstart, or not anything—I owe it to my own Kentucky hill-land and to my people who have inhabited these hills for generations. My hills have given me bread. They have put song in my heart to sing. They have made my brain thirst for knowledge so much that I went beyond my own dark hills to get book knowledge. But I got an earthly degree at home from my own dark soil. I got a degree about birds, cornfields, trees, wildflowers, log shacks, my own people, valleys, and rivers and mists in the valleys—scenes of a fairyland childhood that no college under the sun could teach me.

I have learned from walking through the woods in W-Hollow at night where the wind soughs through the pine tops. I have learned where the big oak trees and the persimmon trees are; I have learned where the blackberry thickets are, where the wild strawberries grow, where the wild crabapple trees blossom in the spring. I have learned where the large rocks are in the fields, where to find the red fox and the gray fox, where the squirrels keep their young in the hollow treetops, and where the quail hides her nest. I know the little secrets of nature, of the wildlife that leads me to these things. I have tried to write about them in my humble, crude fashion. I have enjoyed doing it more than I have eating food, visiting people or cities. My love is with my own soil and my own people.

Slowly, in my own house on my own soil in my own country, I regained my strength and my health. And then I surprised everyone and I surprised myself. Once again, I became a schoolman. I was invited to take over my old school, McKell, again. McKell had gone downhill in the years since I had been principal there. We had had a fine school there in the early thirties, in spite of our problems, but things had changed in 1956. There was a new generation; there were new problems; there was a weak, watered-down curriculum; there were Kentucky teachers leaving the state by the thousands for better-paying jobs in the North; there was an overcrowded building; there was no school spirit among the youth at McKell. McKell had gone down sadly.

The superintendent asked me if I would take over my old school once again and help out. I consulted my doctor. I consulted my wife. My doctor approved. My wife did not. I approved. And I went back to McKell that fall of 1956 as principal.

Remembering Teachers

IN AUGUST of 1952 Jesse Stuart joined the Methodist Church, and was attending Sunday school fairly regularly by the time of his massive heart attack on 8 October 1954. Throughout 1953, he continued to improve his land, write, and travel the lecture circuit at breakneck speed. Honors, including honorary degrees, continued to come his way, but he was living by the clock. In early February of 1954, he began to complain about his health. After suffering severe chest pains, he checked into King's Daughters Hospital for a complete examination only to be told that his problem was muscular. The chest pains did not subside, however, and following a lecture in Murray, Kentucky, on 8 October, he toppled forward into unconsciousness. The time had come for seriously contemplating death as the other side of life, and the result was that when *The Year of My Rebirth* was published in 1956, a number of its reviewers proclaimed it the most autobiographical of Stuart's books.

In the prologue to *The Year of My Rebirth*, Stuart explains his reasons for writing his book as a journal:

I started writing this, my first journal, on January 1, 1955, for two reasons. As a result of my heart attack my hands had become stiff and sore. Dr. Vidt suggested that I gently squeeze and fondle a rubber ball to loosen them up. . . .

The second reason was my wife, Naomi Deane. She urged me to write it. Later she told me why. For weeks she had watched me lying in bed, staring at the ceiling, sometimes refusing to talk, examining my bleak future and wondering if it wouldn't have been better if my heart had stopped beating altogether. . . .

But the prologue begins with, "One day in April of 1955, I found myself in pursuit of the first butterfly of spring." As the prologue indicates, after the heart attack Stuart underwent the dream sensations or visions that would continue in later years and supply the structural technique for *The Kingdom Within*. Throughout *The Year of My Rebirth*, however, Stuart as a heart attack patient is chasing the illusive "first butterfly of spring" in religious terms. Thus he can write, "The idea of resurrection is a most fascinating one. I am glad that Christ's resurrection came in spring. It couldn't have happened in a more likely month than April, judging from the part of earth where I was born and grew to manhood."

Finding his evidence for resurrection in the natural world, Stuart calls for a life of faith: "Now there is another part of this resurrection. It is faith. Do we have faith and do we believe? I never had any trouble having faith. I know I have faith when I see one of the first wild flowers, trailing arbutus, emerge from the cold sod above the rock cliffs. When I see this exquisite flower and the little sweet-potato leaves on its stem, I know that this is trailing arbutus. I am sure of myself. I am positive. I know who I am, where I am, why I am. This is positive identification, and this is positive faith." Statements like this caused some reviewers to refer to *The Year of My Rebirth* as a sermon when it appeared in 1956, but more often than not reviewers agreed with the sentiments of Victor P. Hass of Chicago that Thoreau would have liked Stuart's book (*Chicago Sunday Tribune*, 9 Dec. 1956).

That *The Year of My Rebirth* was intensely introspective should have surprised no one, and those reviewers who quibbled about the writer's using previously published materials failed to see that for Stuart synthesis had become more valuable than analysis in shaping his final vision of man's place in the universe. It was after his journey through "the valley of the shadow" in 1954 that Stuart began shaping his vision of "the whole," a vision fully and admirably articulated in the dream-vision structure of *The Kingdom Within*. What some reviewers failed to see was that Stuart was engaged in expressing that faith which is "another part of this resurrection." Merely to declare that his writing declined after the heart attack is to miss the excitement found in the new direction his writing actually took.

For the most part, reviews of *The Year of My Rebirth* were positive. Although Grimes Caywood noted that it contained previously published anecdotes (*Lexington Herald-Leader*, 2 December 1956), Clyde C. Ball commented on the effectiveness of the use of flashback as a technique (*Huntington Herald-Dispatch*, 1 December 1956). Joe Creason thought it might be Stuart's best-written book because of the effectiveness of the recovery theme as unifying device (*Louisville Courier-Journal*, 2 December 1956), and Artemisia B. Bryson liked it because it "reflects the thinking of a man who has walked a way with Death" (*Fort Worth Star-Telegram*, 16 December 1956). William Hogan saw the book as a record of Stuart's learning to forget old ambitions (*San Francisco Chronicle*, 3 December 1956); John Frye credited Stuart with unusual powers of observation (*Columbus Evening Dispatch*, 23 December 1956); John McManus saw it as valuable because of the example it set for others who had survived a brush with death (*Detroit News*, 30 November 1956); and Sterling North compared the recovery described in *Year* to the raising of Lazarus (*New York World Telegram and Sun*, 30 November 1956). Richard C. Pettigrew compared the genius of Stuart to that of Thoreau (*Birmingham News*, 18 November 1956), and Randall Stewart thought the book an allegory and a symbol rather than the story of a mere man (*Nashville Tennessean*, 2 December 1956). As one anonymous reviewer put it, the value of *The Year of My Rebirth* lies in its being a "warm and wise human document" (*San Francisco Call-Bulletin*, 1 December 1956).

Whatever its merits to the reviewers may have been, the value of *The Year of My Rebirth* to heart attack victims throughout America remains inestimable. Where else can one find such optimism in the face of death? Where else can one find such an honest confession of what it means to be mortal? "Remembering Teachers" is included here not because Stuart's teachers figured directly in his recovery from his heart attack, but because they had so prepared him for the ultimate test of faith that he could say yes to all of life with profound conviction.

I stood down at the end of our walk and looked for a large, light-green automobile with an Ohio license. I knew C.C. (Calvin Clarke) would be here. He was always as good as his word, and he had told us he was coming. His visiting our house for dinner was an occasion for us. Particularly now, at the end of this year that started in pain and depression and ends in health and hope. If it hadn't been for Calvin Clarke's advice over the years, I would not have been able to weather the storm.

Naomi had dinner ready and waiting. My mind went back

through the years as I watched eagerly for him. I had known C.C. since 1912. He was my first teacher, and he became my friend for life. It was he who taught me to read and to write. How could I ever forget him? My father was the district school trustee at Plum Grove then. He recommended this small, slender eighteen-year-old high school graduate. Little did we children know then that we were going to school to a man who would create a legend some day.

He was born on Cedar Creek on the Leftfork of Beaver in Floyd County, at that time 139 miles from a railway station. When he was six, his mother died. He can remember seeing six men lower her homemade coffin into a sandstone grave in the Newsome Cemetery, named for his mother's people. Here the graves of his ancestors were covered with little wooden houses, a few of which still stand.

Theopolis Clarke kept his three small children, Calvin and two younger sisters, together. They lived in a small shack at the foot of a mountain. Here the children attended a rural school, but it wasn't long before Calvin had learned all his teacher could teach him. Then, one day, at his great-uncle's country store on Robinson Creek, he overheard his uncle state that all lawyers went to hell.

"I decided right then I wanted to be a lawyer to see," he told me years later.

He walked a hundred and fifty miles to his grandfather's farm in Greenup County. A cousin, Jack Burke, was living with his grandfather on this large Sandy River-bottom farm, and he persuaded the old man, Jack Newsome, to let this runaway grandson stay and go to school with him. Their grandfather liked the idea of having two grandsons instead of one; so Calvin stayed, worked on his grandfather's farm in summers, and established one of the three highest scholastic records in Greenup High School's 107-year history.

After high school, he took a teacher's examination and made the highest grade in Kentucky. But because of his slight build, too many of the county trustees were afraid to recommend him. They thought he was too young and too small to discipline the large boys. But my father liked him from the first. He recommended him, and he was hired by the five members of the Greenup County Board of Education for the school at Plum Grove.

Calvin Clarke had pupils older and larger than he when he taught his first and second years at Plum Grove. The people who feared he couldn't discipline them because of his small physical stature were stunned to see him at work in a classroom. He had the best-disciplined school in Greenup County. And the people of Plum Grove, children and parents, who were here when he taught school, have never forgotten him.

He was the most alive young man I ever knew. He kept discipline at Plum Grove without ever raising his voice and didn't waste a minute teaching his fifty-six classes in a six-hour day. He brought scissors and hand clippers to the school, and at lunch and recess he cut our hair. There was a root of a big whiteoak elbowing up from the earth, and it was here we used to sit for these free haircuts. He brought needles to school and picked the honey-locust thorns from our feet. He organized us in one year's time into an efficient, disciplined, and enthusiastic school that met with other rural schools and won a consecutive string of fifty arithmetic and spelling matches. As a teacher, C.C. was that good.

From teaching he went to business college, from business college to work for the Shelby Shoe Company in Portsmouth (of which he is now a director), then to Washington and a civil service job, and finally a master's degree, a law degree, and a thriving private practice in Portsmouth that has made him famous in this part of the country. He has practiced before the Supreme Court, and he is said to have the largest real estate holdings in Portsmouth. He was my first teacher in a one-room schoolhouse at Plum Grove, and he has for years handled my financial affairs. His handling of my taxes on the money from *Taps for Private Tussie* is an eight-year story in itself, which I am not at liberty to write down. I can only say that when a government attorney came one last time to try to collect more taxes from me, C.C. collected from him. That's the way it ended.

After 1944, the year I had my greatest financial success, I got a furlough from the Navy to ask C.C. if he would take care of my taxes. This was the first time I'd earned enough to employ an attorney. Heretofore, I'd made out my own income-tax returns, and I hadn't exactly overflowed Treasury Department coffers with my contributions. But getting C.C. was a most important move for me. I have learned since how lucky I have been these last twelve years to have C.C. saving a part of my earnings for me.

When my novel was selected by a book club and bought by MGM in the same year, it was announced in all the papers that I had struck it rich. In no time I had everybody coming to sell me insurance, property, automobiles, houses, and coal mines, to ask me for endowments for colleges, donations for churches, and all kinds of personal loans. Had I given ten dollars to each request, I wouldn't have had anything left. I got letters from old friends who were in "dire" circumstances and in "desperate" need of help. I got letters from people wanting me to finance their get-rich-quick schemes, profits from which we would share jointly. One friend and classmate wanted me to buy a theater for him. When C.C. asked him what security he could give, he replied, "I can't give him any security, but he can be my silent partner."

When these letters came to me, I sent them to C.C. When a man came wanting to borrow eighty grand to start a super garage, I sent him to C.C. I sent them all to C.C., for he took a special delight in handling my problems and telling these people that I didn't really have as much money as there was gold buried at Fort Knox.

They came away from C.C.'s office in Portsmouth, Ohio, a disappointed lot. They didn't believe what he told them about my financial situation. They started wild rumors that he, already a man of considerable wealth, was doing all his business with my money. I let C.C. explain my affairs to these schemers, dreamers, and that little handful of friends always in "dire circumstances" in whatever way he wanted to. After he got through with them, they never came to me again. I don't know what he told them. But I do believe he could have made straight "A's" in psychology without ever opening a book.

A few of these people who wanted to do business with my money bear mentioning. One had the idea of building a "casino" on the Sandy River, where he would have floor shows, an orchestra, expensive foods and wines, roulette wheels, crap tables, and slot machines. For his site he had chosen a farm which had a family cemetery of about twenty graves on it that would have to be removed. "But I won't let a little graveyard of twenty graves stand in my way," he told me. This fellow, as my friend of many years and a local politician, wanted to borrow a mere $450,000 from me for this project. I sent him to see C.C. in a hurry. The next time I saw this man, he smiled, spoke in a friendly way, and apologized to me because he was too late in getting this loan, which was "too big for the local bank to make."

Besides my classmate who wanted me to buy him a $30,000 theater, I had parents of several "talented" young men and women who wanted me to finance their children through colleges and universities. One of my former students wanted me to buy him a country newspaper with a circulation of 1,900 for $26,000. C.C. enjoyed lecturing this one on economics, so he told me later. A house that a man wanted to sell me for $28,000, "not a penny less," sold later for $14,000. A casual acquaintance who was building an expensive yacht to launch on the Ohio River wanted to borrow $10,000 from me to pay the mortgage on his home.

It took about four years for the word to get around that I had an attorney who wasn't willing to loan my money because he had borrowed it all himself. Nevertheless, when the American Legion Hall burned down in Greenup, they came to me to borrow money to rebuild it instead of going to the bank. Finally, the many people who had been coming to me in a steady stream seeking money slowed down to a trickle.

Had it not been for C.C.'s handling all this, I don't know what I would have done. It got to the point where I couldn't do any work because of all the people who came, like the Tussies, wanting something. We would come home in the evenings to find people sitting on our front porch waiting to borrow money or to interest me in a financial proposition. Several of these people we had to keep all night. Later I learned better and hauled them back to Greenup to let them find their own places to stay.

I had a few ideas about investing what was left after taxes in 1944, the year I was supposed to have made a million dollars. I wanted C.C. to invest it in one thing. "Leave it to me," he said, shaking his head. "I'll guarantee you won't lose anything. But I won't put all your eggs in one basket." So I left all the investments up to him. And every investment he made for me was safe and has made a reasonable amount of money.

Once, after I'd seen how much worry and trouble a little money can be, I got the idea that I would give every dollar of it to the State of Kentucky for bookmobiles. My correspondence with C.C. will show I had this idea long before this state got bookmobiles.

Said C.C., "No, I'm not for your spending all you have for bookmobiles. You might get sick and not be able to work. Then what would you do?"

"Not I," I answered, laughing at him. "I'll be able to work a full day until I'm eighty."

But leave it to my friend C.C. to be right. In less than six years I had collapsed of a heart attack. And if it hadn't been for his wise handling of my financial affairs, I don't know what we would have done when hospital and doctor bills mounted up and I had to stop working.

Once I rebelled on him and bought $3,500 worth of cattle against his advice. I fed these cattle three barn lofts of good hay and all that I had stacked in my fields, besides a lot of grain. Then I hired a man to feed and care for my cattle when I was away on lecture tours. After keeping these cattle a year, I sold them for less than I bought them for. C.C. had warned me not to buy, feed, and sell cattle at that time. He was right again. He suggested that I write short stories about cattle instead. I did—enough to pay this deficit.

Then he suggested that I stop raising wheat, chickens, and even tobacco. He suggested that I wasted too much time farming that I should use writing. After losing $309 in a year on two hundred chickens, a crop of tobacco that heated after it was bulked down in the barn, and a wheat crop that I couldn't thresh because the hills were too steep for the combine, I decided to listen to C.C. I rented my tobacco base and sold my chickens.

Why did I call on him to handle my taxes? He used to make me toe the mark when I went to school to him. He switched me for fighting three times in one week. I went back to him because I had never been away. I had never forgotten him from the first day he taught me. No one could forget him. Why did the Greenup County's Superintendent of Schools, Johnnie Prichard, give him his first school? When C.C. was a shine boy in Greenup, Kentucky, trying to make himself a few extra dimes, it was Johnnie Prichard's old rundown shoes he used to shine so well they looked like new.

C.C. has never used tobacco in any form nor drunk intoxicating liquors. He never forgets a name, a face, a property value, a telephone number. One morning C.C. came to Greenup on a tax case. He was rushing as usual, but he recognized Little Bob

Griffith, one of his former Plum Grove pupils, loafing on the street.

"There's something I want to ask you, Little Bob," he said, after they had greeted each other for the first time in thirty-eight years. "I want to know if you were the one who slipped those rotten eggs in Roy Perkins' pocket and he sat down on them in school?"

"Yes, I did, Mr. Clarke," Little Bob admitted. "But I was afraid to confess it to you then."

"Did you carry the steps from the Plum Grove School to the foot of the hill on Halloween night in 1912?"

"No, Mr. Clarke, it wasn't me that time," Little Bob said proudly.

"I always wanted to clear these two things up," C.C. said.

After C.C. had gone, Little Bob turned to me and said, "He's the greatest teacher I ever had. Think about him remembering the schoolhouse steps and the eggs! And think about a man as busy and important as he is who would stop and talk to me for ten minutes on the street."

One night at our house I was kidding C.C. about the possibilities of his going to hell.

"I'll never forget," he answered, "what my uncle said when I was a little boy. He said that after a lawyer took his last breath, he went straight to hell. When I got to be a lawyer, I said to myself, 'Here will be one honest lawyer. Here will be one who wants to see his ancestors on the other side after he leaves this world.'"

Yesterday Naomi and I were driving two Texas friends of ours, C.E. and Flossie Bryant, around the valley when Flossie suddenly pointed to the hills and shouted, "Look! Look at that goldenrod. Isn't it beautiful! I've never seen so much!"

Now this was strange talk to us. I guess we don't think much about our goldenrod, there's so much of it. But the talk got even stranger when C.E. said, "Yes, Flossie loves it. How much do you pay for goldenrod in Texas, Flossie?"

"A dollar twenty for a dozen stems."

Down in Texas they *paid* for goldenrod! Naomi and I roared with laughter at the idea. That was like paying for dandelions, or cut grass. Naomi and I decided we'd export goldenrod to Texas and make a million. We all had fun with the idea.

Goldenrod has always reminded me of Robert Burns, and for a

good reason. Years back I laid a sprig of Kentucky goldenrod on Robert Burns' grave, near Dumfries, Scotland.

In the spring of 1937 I received a Guggenheim Fellowship to travel to Europe. I was delighted. Not only would this be my first time to travel on the ocean and to be away from my native country, but it would give me a chance to pay tribute to Robert Burns. Although he had been dead for 141 years, he was the man who had made this trip possible for me. I had read the prose and poetry of hundreds of other English, Scottish, Irish, and European writers and I had made friends among them, but the writer who meant the most to me was Robert Burns.

When I entered Greenup High School, I had never heard of Robert Burns. But my English teacher, Mrs. Robert Hatton, whose maiden name was Hattie MacFarland and who was of Scottish descent, grew up reading Robert Burns. Her father always kept a volume of Burns' poems close by and read them aloud to his family. And when Mrs. Hatton loaned me her book of poems by Robert Burns, I was so delighted I put everything else aside to read it.

Robert Burns' poetry caused me to make low grades in high school. I read his poems and neglected to work at my math, history, science, and even my English. But now this thought was often in my mind: If this man, Robert Burns, a Scottish plowboy who was born in a poor home and never had many opportunities, could grow up to write poetry that would endure, why can't I? I am of Scottish descent, I was born in a one-room shack in the Kentucky hills, and I, too, plow the soil. Why can't I do it if Burns could?

This was the way I felt about it. Mrs. Hatton and I discussed Robert Burns during the noon hours and after school. I told Mrs. Hatton that Robert Burns' River Ayr was my Sandy River and his River Nith was my Tygart. My father's farm in W-Hollow became Robert Burns' father's farm at Alloway, and there was a Highland Mary in our Greenup High School. Robert Burns was within my reach. We were born under the same circumstances. His language, once the dialect was removed, was the simple language we spoke in the Kentucky hills. Robert Burns was a peasant poet.

Not only could I understand him, but I could move him, his house, poetry, everything from the far country of Scotland, to my Kentucky hills. I could do this though he had been dead over a century. For I understood Burns better than I did many of the native American writers I was forced to study. I told Mrs. Hatton how I felt about this poet, Robert Burns. I never got through thanking her for the book she loaned me.

"Since you like Robert Burns so well," she told me one day at noon, "I want to make you a present of this volume of Burns' collected poems."

This book changed my life. On my way to school in the mornings, five miles over rough terrain, somewhere along the path I would sit under the autumn trees and read Robert Burns. Even in winter I'd sit on a stump, log, or stone and read Robert Burns. I liked to read "The Cotter's Saturday Night" in winter. I liked to read "The shortning winter-day is near a close," and then look around at how dark it would be getting. Darkness came early, and I had work at home to do. I'd jump up, put my book under my arm, and take off running to get home before dark. I had wood to cut, water to draw from the well, and milking and feeding to do. But now I was usually late doing these chores. Sometimes I'd get mad at myself, for I had once been industrious. I had been until I got acquainted with Robert Burns.

It was in the springtime of the year that Burns did most to me. He made me forget to cut wood and carry water and feed and milk. For I walked along the road with Highland Marys and Bonnie Jeans. We had the Holy Willies and the Highland Harrys, too. A century didn't separate Burns and me. He spoke in a fresh, close voice to me from the pages of his book.

I was never by myself. Though my dog might hunt away to find a possum, Burns was always with me. He hunted with me, plowed near me, and walked over my hills with me. I had found a literary man, although I didn't think of him as such, who was shaping and making a new life for me. For I, too, was writing poems. If Burns could sing of his neighbors, I could sing of mine. I wanted to write poems like his though, poems that sang. He didn't have to struggle to write them. They wrote themselves.

Burns was with me through my early years, and he went to college and various universities with me. By now I had found other literary companions, older fellows compared to Burns. Burns was always young. He never grew old. And I would have to grow old indeed, senile in fact, before I turned away from the youthful living of Robert Burns. There might come the time when we would part, but it wasn't in sight yet. To be young and happy and full of life, love, and sorrow was to be like Burns. Burns woke the song in me, he made me write *Man with a Bull-Tongue Plow*.

Because Mrs. Hatton had given me a collection of Robert Burns' poems in high school, I was riding an English ship across the ocean in 1937. Two published books had earned me a Guggenheim Fellowship. Robert Burns could never come to my country, so I was going to his. And I had the idea that if Burns knew how many writers he had inspired, how many people he had made happy and made love poetry almost a century and a half after his death, he would surely be a happy poet where he dwelled in the skies. Once when I was a junior in high school, I dreamed that I died and saw Shakespeare in the clouds. He and Milton were talking together, aloof from everybody, and I couldn't reach either. But Burns had a whole crowd around him, and he wasn't any trouble to meet. He was a regular fellow with a good sense of humor.

Scotland was cold, green, beautiful country with stone houses and fences and sea gulls gliding over Greenock and flying mists floating low over the grassy hilltops north of the Clyde. Robert Burns' Auld Reekie was still Auld Reekie. Smoke clouds scooted over the housetops and the stacks which protected the homes from downdrafts. Smoke clouds scooted on the low sea winds out to the Firth-of-Forth. This was Robert Burns' land. Robert Burns had once walked these streets of Edinburgh. He had once been wined and dined the hero of the hour here. Now I was going to pay to Robert Burns my simple tribute from the hills of Kentucky.

After getting used to Scotland's temperamental weather, its foods, currency, tobacco, language, and people, none of whom I knew as well as Robert Burns and not a one as friendly toward me, I set off by rail to Glasgow and by bus from there to Alloway. This was midsummer, and tourists were arriving by the thousands in the Burns country. Now I learned that a poet who had never made more than 3,500 American dollars in his whole lifetime, who died penniless, was the greatest earning power for the poor people of Southeast Scotland. People were coming from all over the world to see the land of Robert Burns, from America, Canada, South America, from all over Europe, Africa, Asia, Australia, New Zealand. Robert Burns had spoken to others besides this plowboy from Kentucky. Robert Burns was universal, he spoke to and for all mankind.

I waited my turn to see the inside of the house at Alloway where he was born. I was deeply touched by the barnlike structure, with low doors and small windows, framed with stone. This house had sheltered a great man. And at the same time one portion of it had housed the cattle and kept them warm on that night of his birth, January 25, 1759. I visited the remains of Alloway's Kirk, which figures in "Tam O'Shanter," and I saw the Auld Brigg. I saw the graves of Burns' ancestors buried around Alloway Kirk. I visited Mount Oliphant, Kirkosweld and Lochlea, where Burns lived seven years of his life.

Everywhere I carried his volume of collected poems. This was not the one Mrs. Hutton had given me. I had worn it out. I had worn out a second volume, for I had carried Burns with me even when I plowed in the fields or drove the team to Greenup. I had carried Robert Burns to the steel mills, to the army camp, and to college. I kept Robert Burns in my own library and in all the high school libraries where I had taught. I had the brief journey of his life well memorized. Now I was visiting his places and taking my time about it. The land Burns plowed was sacred earth. The crude old stone houses where he lived and the taverns where he drank and the fields where he walked were what I had traveled far to see.

I went to Mossgiel, where he had spent four years of his brief life. It was here he failed as a farmer, but not as a poet. Here he wrote many of his finest lyrics, including "The Cotter's Saturday Night." Then I went to Mauchline, where I spent a week. Here Robert Burns and Jean Armour went to housekeeping. And in the churchyard, many of Robert Burns's contemporaries slept, their graves pointed out now because Burns immortalized them in his verse. There must not have been any libel laws in those days. Maybe some people living today would have greater prospects for immortality if the possibilities for libel against writers were reduced.

In Kilmarnock, where I thought I found the poorest people in Scotland, Burns was as much alive as he was in his lifetime. In every home and shop, regardless how poor the family, there was always a picture of Robert Burns. He was on the walls. He was on the dishes.

let a pupil down if she thought he was in the right, and she never let him down if she knew he was wrong but thought he had possibilities of becoming a better person.

For instance, one of Lena's "sweet little girls" was assaulted by two brothers from a family of influence and power in town. The girl's people were of humble origin but had a reputation for uprightness and wholesomeness in the community. Yet this case couldn't even get to trial until Lena Wells stepped in. She went to the aid of her schoolgirl, who had just graduated from high school. Much money was spent, the case was forced into the open, and in a trial that was long remembered the boys from the influential family were convicted.

She is loyal to her own political party, but if one of her boys is on the opposite ticket and is running for a local or state office, she will go to help him. She is a fluent speaker, and she learned political strategy early from her father and brothers. She has entered the political arena most forcefully when she thought corruption was dominant. She has been the deciding factor in local primaries in eliminating candidates whose integrity was doubtful.

"Yes, it was time to rid this country of old politicians that lived from the courthouse," she said. "I asked one of my good boys to run to eliminate corruption and waste of the taxpayers' money. He agreed, on the condition that I help him. I got out and went all over the county. He was elected, and the people like him so well he will be elected again. Now I have had to warn him about waste and corruption."

One of her favorites was a Jewish boy whose father was a business competitor of her husband's. But such a little thing as business didn't matter when she had a bright boy whom she thought might have a promising future. When he finished high school, she had a college selected for him and, as she did with many of her other boys and girls, she went with him to make application. But the college dean told Mrs. Voiers that they had enrolled their quota and had excessive applications on the waiting list. Mrs. Voiers then went to another college, where she heard the same story. She went to a third, the oldest college in Kentucky, and he was accepted. Mrs. Voiers learned later that the two institutions that refused this boy had accepted students with lesser qualifications who applied after he did.

"I blew my top," she said. "I knew there was prejudice. I figured the deans of both institutions were lying and looking me straight in the eyes when they did it. I kicked up an awful fuss. Then I got him in the third college, which was the best of the three anyway. I showed them his school record, told them that he was a fine boy and I believed he'd be a great executive someday."

As I walked the ridge path with Lena Wells that January afternoon thirty-three years ago, when she was twenty-six and I was fifteen, she told me that I would write a book someday if I worked hard enough. And she told me that she would always keep in touch with me. That moment I had my first stirrings of ambition to try to amount to something in life, simply because she had so much confidence in me. But I thought when I left Greenup High School and she went back to her home town, Vanceburg, that we would not see each other again.

Yet a couple of years later, when I was working at the steel mills, there was a call at my boardinghouse.

"Stuart, a fine-looking dame to see you."

I went downstairs to the lobby, and there sat Lena Wells.

"Thought I'd drop by to see if you planned to enter college," she said.

"I plan to enter in September," I told her. "That's only a few days away. I made up my mind to go a while back and I've saved what money I could."

"I knew you would," she said.

When I came home from Lincoln Memorial, she rode over to W-Hollow to check on my activities. When I taught my first one-room high school, Miss Lykins came to visit. When she read anything about me in the paper or one of my stories in a magazine, I'd get a letter, "I'm proud of you. I always told you you could do it." When one of the algebra students I was teaching won a state-wide competition, she wrote me, "See what I told you. See how right I was! You'll make a better math teacher than an English teacher, because math was so hard for you to learn."

Then I entered Vanderbilt University to do graduate work. One day after lunch at the Wesley Hall Cafeteria, I was back in the steam and heat of the dishwashing room when someone spoke, "Well, well, look where I find you. Up among the clouds as always." It was Miss Lykins all right, only she was now Mrs. Voiers, and her husband, Gus, was with her.

When I became Greenup County School Superintendent, Mrs. Voiers wrote me letters. She visited me. When my first book was published, she was jubilant. When my name appeared in *Who's Who in America*, she even noticed that, and wrote me a long letter. When each of my books appeared, she read it and reported her opinions, good and bad, back to me. When I got a Guggenheim Fellowship, Mrs. Voiers was there to see me off, saying, "Go to Europe and travel in every country you can."

Everyone will tell you that to see Lena Wells coming puts new life, hope, and ambition in a man, that to listen to her gives him a renewed faith in his future. This is the way she has taught and still teaches, with great faith and fervor. It has proved fortunate for thousands that Lena Wells chose the great profession of teaching. More than any other teacher I know, she has left a permanent stamp on her children.

There are two reasons why I never left home. One, I wanted to teach Kentucky children and lift the standards of learning of my people. Second, I wanted to write of my people, of my beautiful hill country, in my day and time. I wanted to record this country's scenes, its tempo and customs, the troubles and desires of its people, just as man photographs his children through the different ages of their lives.

My first college English teacher, Harry Harrison Kroll, of Lincoln Memorial University, told me back in 1927, when I was a sophomore there, I should return to my own country after I finished college. He told me to write of my own people. He said, "There are things in your own back yard that need to be written." Harry Harrison Kroll hadn't written a book at that time. Since then he has written seventeen novels, one biography, and his own autobiography. He is a wise man, and he knew what he was talking about.

Four years later, when I was doing graduate work at Vanderbilt University, Donald Davidson, a great teacher, a fine poet and critic, went over certain of my poems. He particularly liked those I had done about my people and my country. He revised one for me, "Elegy for Mitch Stuart," which sold to *The American Mercury* while H.L. Mencken was still the editor. "Go back to your country and write of your own people," Donald Davidson told me. "There is where your heart is. You put feeling into what you write about the people you know in your own country. You remind me so much of the Irish writers in your love for your own soil. Go back and write about what you know the best."

I never forgot what these two writers, who were my teachers and close personal friends, told me. I came back to my Greenup County hills, where I wrote *Man with a Bull-Tongue Plow* within the first eleven months after I had left Vanderbilt.

While I was teaching, writing, and farming here, I was offered a position teaching English in a high school in Oklahoma. I was also offered a teaching job in faraway Portland, Maine, another in a high school in West Virginia. But when I thought about leaving here, even for double my salary, at a time when I needed money to buy writing paper and clothes, something held me here. I couldn't leave. Yet I thought if I were offered something better, I still might go.

In 1937, when I was in England, I visited the late Edward J. O'Brien at 8 Waterloo Place, London. There I was approached for a tryout in British movies. A director liked my looks, my voice, and accent, and thought these would go over well in the British Isles. But I was not interested in this offer. I was a writer, not an actor. At least I thought and hoped I was a writer. So I refused to be photographed. I wasn't cut out to be an actor.

Before I left the British Isles in 1938, I had a brief part on a BBC program which was broadcast all through the British Commonwealth and to her territories over the world. I got letters from every place, with the result that I was offered a program on BBC just to tell stories of the people in my native Kentucky hills. But something drew me back to this side of the Atlantic. Stronger than gravity, it was W-Hollow that pulled me back.

In 1940, when I was put on a program in Hollywood with a half-dozen other speakers, we were each allowed four minutes. I spoke an hour. They applauded me. They told me to keep on going. I was offered a radio program in Hollywood after this talk. I wondered why they liked to hear me speak so much when each man on the program was better known and had accomplished more than I had. One had written thirty books. I had written four at that time.

I figured the reason they liked me was because I had remained true to my country. Maybe I had held on to what these men had lost. They were making money so big the figures staggered me.

They made my head swim. I was making hardly enough to live. But I had held onto my heritage without exploiting it. So I didn't take this radio program with a big salary and a promise of something bigger. Naomi, who was with me, wondered if I had acted wisely. But something told me to return to Kentucky. I came home and became a city-school superintendent on an $1,800-a-year salary while I wrote *Taps for Private Tussie*.

During the war another offer came through which floored me. I was offered a thousand dollars a week to be a script writer in Hollywood. Instead, after dieting and resting to bring my blood pressure down from 196, I joined the Navy. I didn't belong in Hollywood anyway. I knew that.

Then, after my discharge, I was offered a position teaching creative writing at Columbia University, where I had been speaking. This offer was very interesting. Writing for me had come to a standstill after the war. Two years away from my native land had done something to me. I couldn't sell anything I wrote. I was ashamed of everything I put on paper. I wondered what Manhattan would do for me. I was tempted by this offer. I even inquired about housing and learned it was difficult to get. But then, when the decision had to be made, there was that something here in Kentucky that held me. I was a small puppet tied to a string, and my native land held the other end and pulled me back every time I tried to escape.

Since the publication of my book describing my teaching experiences, *The Thread That Runs So True*, I have been offered teaching positions at Iowa State Teachers College, Baylor University, the University of Nevada, the University of California, the University of South Carolina, and elsewhere. Each time I considered, or thought I did, but each time my high prison hills—bleak and lonely in winter, bright with butterflies and wild flowers in spring and summer, and filled with a thousand shades of brilliant leaf colors in autumn—pulled me back.

Going back over the years, I have tried to answer the question so often asked me: Why have you remained here when you could do so much better elsewhere? But could I have done better elsewhere? What if I had gone to teach in Oklahoma, West Virginia, or Maine? What would I be doing now, I wonder. What if I had become an actor in the British Isles and become a British subject? Or if I had become a radio personality or gone to Hollywood as a script writer? Why have I been offered these things? I can answer this now. My country has been my fountainhead, my source, my inspiration, my everything. These people didn't want me. They wanted my land through me.

The man I am, my country was helped to make and shape. I ate food grown from this thin soil. I breathed winds that blew over cone-shaped hills and down deep valleys. I am the seed of my father and mother, whose home was these hills. I cannot desert what has made me. I tell people there's something in the land that won't let me leave and that I am nothing without the land. This is the truest answer I know.

The School Bell
Rings Again

AFTER HIS heart attack at Murray, Kentucky, on 8 October 1954, Stuart had recuperated enough to return to McKell High School as principal in the fall of 1956. The story of that principalship was published as *Mr. Gallion's School* in 1967. It might be better to say that the book was based upon that principalship, for the reviewers seemed not to know what to say about the work. Some praised it highly, but others contended that it fell far short of such earlier works as *The Thread That Runs So True*.

It is true that in the 1960s Stuart's life was as busy as the decade was stormy for the nation at large. After serving as visiting lecturer at American University in Cairo, Egypt (1961-62), he served as writer in residence at Eastern Kentucky University (1965-66). He traveled in Europe in 1964, and he toured Africa and Europe in 1969. He had become a world figure with numerous honorary degrees to his credit, a number of which came in the decade of the sixties: Marshall University (1962), Northern Michigan University (1964), Eastern Kentucky University (1964), Berea College (1966), Murray State University (1968), and Pfeiffer College (1969). Throughout the decade he published voluminously, including no fewer than fifteen books. Book-length studies about Stuart also appeared, including Everetta Love Blair's *Jesse Stuart: His Life and Works* (Columbia: University of South Carolina Press, 1967), Lee Pennington's *The Dark Hills of Jesse Stuart* (Cincinnati: Harvest Press, 1967), Ruel E. Foster's *Jesse Stuart* (New York: Twayne, 1968), and Mary Washington Clarke's *Jesse Stuart's Kentucky* (New York: McGraw-Hill, 1968). At the close of the decade, the second edition of Hensley C. Woodbridge's bibliography of Stuart's works was published—*Jesse and Jane Stuart: A Bibliography* (Murray, Kentucky: Murray State University, 1969)—the first edition having been published in 1960.

On 29 May 1967, Stuart spoke to the graduating class of Murray State University on the topic "Rebels With a Cause." In that speech he made quite clear his purpose in *Mr. Gallion's School* by relating incidents from the life of Quintus Horatius Flaccus (Horace), Roman satirist who lived from 65 to 8 B.C. He explained that Horace changed his approach for handling dissension in his time by praising that which was strong rather than attacking that which was weak: "After Augustus became emperor, there was still dissension in the land and here is where the influence of Horace was so great. For Horace, a deeply religious man, was obedient to the gods he knew. He had changed from his early protest poems, his heartless poems, to write poetry of the sturdy Roman family, the great yeomanry of the land, that sturdy citizenry that was the pillar upon which the Roman empire drew its strength." Having made his case for Horace, Stuart then told his audience: "Today our country is at war, our third war in twenty-five years of national scale, under the auspices of fighting for the freedom of other people that would, if not for us, be suppressed. But the fact is, we are at war. And another fact is, we have dissension in our land, a kind that Horace and Emperor Augustus knew in the Roman Empire. Our dissension might even be worse in our republic, a land I love and of which I am proud to be a citizen."

Stuart went on to discuss our national dissension and to discuss his last year as principal at McKell High School. Much of the dissension he found at McKell High School came, he concluded, from a movie called "Rebel Without a Cause," starring James Dean: "Very soon we had so many boys going around, mad about nothing, trying to be James Deans, that I went to see the movie that had influenced them. The trend was mad at the world for nothing." Believing James Dean's "flimsy celluloid content" emphasized the wrong things, Stuart went to work creating his own character, George Gallion, who would emphasize the right things. Our dissension in the sixties, he argued, came from within and forced all of us into being rebels either with a cause or without one: "Why be a rebel without a cause when there are so many good causes? And the best is never to burn a flag unless you have a better one." "Horace is very much with us," he told his audience. "He was a writing rebel with a cause and his written word was on the right emphasis."

In *Mr. Gallion's School*, Stuart was also a "writing rebel with a cause." Like Horace, he was out to save the republic—not by attacking its weaknesses, but by cultivating its strengths. This is made clear early in *Mr. Gallion's School*:

> "I told you the world has changed," Grace said. "Your ideas are too old, George."
>
> "Character and discipline are never too old. We've had these for five thousand years."

Thus the anonymous reviewer who objected to *Mr. Gallion's School* because the plot and characters were not true (*Kirkus Reviews*, 1 October 1967) missed the point entirely, as did Walter B. Greenwood with his assertion that the book was an embarrassment to Stuart's many admirers (*Buffalo Evening News*, 9 December 1967). Such epithets as "didactic," "naive," "old-fashioned," and "preachy" neither explain the writer's effort nor his accomplishment. I recognized this when I commented on *Mr. Gallion's School* as promoting a "philosophy of positive displacement" (*Peabody Reflector*, November-December 1967), and Carl May recognized it when he wrote that the book was as close to writing calculated protest as Stuart had come (*Nashville Tennessean*, 26 November 1967). Doris C. Miller realized that the action only "relates" to Stuart's experiences at McKell High School (*Huntington Herald-Advertiser*, 12 November 1967), and Joy Bale saw the book as an expression of concern over "serious values" (*Louisville Courier-Journal*, 12 November 1967). Joseph Caruso saw it not as a novel but as a plea for good teachers and teaching (*Boston Globe*, 3 December 1967), and Marian Garin Gregory found it to be authentic and effective protest (*Fort-Worth Star-Telegram*, 19 November 1967).

George Gallion is not merely another Don Quixote. Gallion has experienced the truth of a former time, and he will not settle for less. And so it is with Jesse Stuart in his Horatian mold. "The School Bell Rings Again," the section included here, comprises chapter 1 of *Mr. Gallion's School*. It is based on Stuart's decision to return to McKell High School as principal.

Puffs of warm July wind came through the car to fan George Gallion's face and his woolly arm that rested on the open window. The car was new and powerful—it had 300 horses under the hood. Grace drove up to the summit of the overpass that spanned the railroad tracks. Directly beneath them, the Ohio River stretched like a white ribbon in the broad green valley.

"How wonderful it is that we're both alive and together, and we don't have to worry about anything any more—except," Grace said, "your health."

"Worry is the worst of all diseases," George said. "It can kill you. I'm not worrying about my health, and don't you worry about it."

They drove on in silence, down the overpass now, onto a straightaway which led into Main Street and the center of Greenwood. It was the first time in two years—since his illness—that George had been here.

Made of dull-gray pavement and colorless brick buildings, Greenwood is one of the oldest towns in Kentucky. Even in this fast-changing mid-twentieth century, most of its 1100 inhabitants are the direct descendants of its first settlers a hundred years ago. Here the mountaineers and the river people still meet, marry, fight, love, die. It was here, too, that so much of George's life had been spent. He remembered the days when Greyhound boats carried passengers on the river and the Negro stevedores sang as they loaded freight. He used to watch huge horses pull loaded draywagons up the steep bank with sparks flying from their steel-shod hooves. He glanced to his left at his wife's old home, standing coolly back from the street, surrounded by elms. He remembered he had walked to school years ago, beside her.

"Here's home, Grace," he said.

"Not any more. The Valley is far dearer to me now."

Down Main Street in the shade of the giant elms, the non-descript houses on either side blocked the Ohio River breezes. Elm leaves hung motionless in wilted clusters from the interlocking elm branches above Main Street. Large elm roots were exposed at the bases of the trees, coiled like huge reptiles enjoying the penciled spots of sunlight that found holes in the canopies of wilted leaves. On the windows and doors that faced the courthouse square were the familiar names of merchants and professional men they knew. Seats donated by the town's local politicians were filled with men who sat, whittled, and talked.

"This old town does look good," George said, smiling. "It's good to see the old names and the familiar houses."

Grace drove around the square up the other side and parked in front of Tad Meadowbrook's barbershop.

Grace got out and hurried around to the other side to open the door for George, but he was already easing himself out slowly. George had both feet on the street and he straightened up slowly while she put a coin in the parking meter. Grace was an attractive woman, tall and slender, with large hazel eyes, a wide thin mouth, and a strong chin. She was in her mid-forties and her once-brown hair brushed back from her face was streaked with gray.

"George, Tad's barbershop is full," she said. "You want to wait or come back later?"

"No, I'll get my hair cut now."

"Yes, I know, you want to hear the gossip."

His blue summer suit was wrinkled and his shoes needed a shine. He was six feet tall with broad shoulders, a short neck, a large head and long deep-set gray eyes.

"You bet I want to hear the gossip. I want to hear some man-talk."

"I'll go in with you."

"Sure you haven't some shopping you'd like to do?"

"Not today," she replied, smiling. "I want to learn why you like barbershop talk!"

As they walked across the sidewalk together she put her hand in his. "It's the best place in the world to hear what's going on," he said. "Tad has more news in an hour than the *Greenwood Times* prints in a week. I'd rather hear Old Tad talk than read the newspapers, anyway. He never slants the news. He's the most authentic reporter in the Tri-State."

"Here's the step," she said. "Go easy! Remember what Dr. Vinn told you."

The barbershop was the bottom half of the square two-story building. There was a big sign on the door in block black letters with red trimming: TAD'S BARBERSHOP. TODDLE IN AND TALK WITH TAD. HE'S THE BEST BARBER YOU EVER HAD.

Tad left the chair where he was cutting the hair of a man George didn't know, came over and opened the door.

"Come in, Professor and Mrs. Professor," he greeted them warmly with a big grin. He held a long cigar between his gold front teeth. "I've been thinking about when I'd get to cut your hair again. It's been a long time since you've been here. How're you feeling, Professor Gallion?"

"Could whip my weight in wildcats," George Gallion said with a wan smile.

"I don't know about now but I remember when you could," said the young man at the other chair. "You sure poured it on me once. Remember?"

"Ken, I didn't recognize you," George said. "You've grown up and lost a lot of hair. You've lost yours and we've held ours, haven't we, Tad? But our hair has changed its color a little."

"Yes, mine used to be black as a stove pot," Tad said, smiling. "Women used to wish for my wavy black hair! Now look. White!"

The stranger in Tad's chair looked at his watch.

"You want a haircut, Professor?" Tad asked. "If you do you'll have to wait awhile!"

"George, maybe we'd better come back later," Grace said.

She looked around at the row of men. The chairs were filled and several were standing. She was the only woman in the shop. On every patch of wall were hung pictures of pin-up girls, many of them dating back to the 1940s. In the corner of the shop were rifles and shotguns Tad traded or sold when he wasn't busy. Near them was his five-string banjo which he would play sitting in his barber's chair when he needed customers. Sometimes people danced in the streets to the dance tunes he played.

"No, I'll wait," George said.

"Then I'll get you some chairs," Ken said.

"Professor, I didn't introduce you to the fellows around here," Tad said as Ken came from the back of the shop with two wooden stools.

"I've always said, Professor, if I could have been with you longer I'd never have been in this shop with Dad cutting hair," Ken said.

"What's wrong with barbering? It's a good profession."

"I want you all to meet my friends, Professor and Mrs. George Gallion." Tad addressed the room at large. "He used to be principal of Kensington High School, and I started cutting his hair then. When he was there we never had all this trouble like we're having down there now. Right, Professor?"

"What's wrong at the school?" George Gallion asked.

"What isn't wrong with it, Professor, would be a better question," Ken said. "The trucks that take soft drinks and milk won't even go there any more! The boys down there rob the trucks! They walk out of the school and just take what they want when a truck comes in."

"You're kidding me."

"No, Ken ain't kiddin' you," Tad said as his scissors now moved swiftly over his customer's head. "He's right, Professor. I still live over in Kensington. That school is the talk of the town. We was just discussing it 'fore you came in. The kids down there tell the teachers what to do. Right in the middle of a class some tough kid'll git up and say to the teacher, 'Now, we've had class in this room for thirty minutes and the next thirty minutes we'll go outside under the shade of them locust trees and finish the class.' And, Professor, they just git. Poor teacher can't do a thing about it!"

"Where is the principal?" George asked. He began biting his lower lip.

"Now, don't you get all worked up over it, George," Grace said. "You're not principal of that school now. It doesn't concern you."

"It does concern me. It concerns everybody."

"Well, there's nothing you can do about it now," she said. "So why worry about it? Leave it to younger principals and teachers."

"They can't find teachers who'll go there and stand the abuse for the low salaries they get," put in one of Tad's customers who was standing near the window.

Seems like I ought to know you, George Gallion thought. He looked at this big square-shouldered man in a business suit. I know I've seen you someplace before.

"Do they have the same people living down there they used to have?" George Gallion asked. "Have all the people I used to know there twenty years ago moved out and strangers moved in? What's the cause of all this trouble?"

"I'd say seventy percent of them are the people you know," Ken said, as his customer stepped down from the chair. "I'd say the youngsters raising all the hell down there are the sons and daughters of the boys and girls you taught there twenty years ago."

"Then I must have done a rotten job," George Gallion said.

"No, Professor, it's not that," Ken said. "They let 'em do as they please. They don't have any discipline. Nobody seems to be interested or to care what goes on. Teachers don't tell them what to do. They tell the teachers!"

"But what about the principal?" George Gallion asked.

"Well, he won't be there this year," Tad said. Tad's customer got down and another stepped into the chair. "They don't have a principal. Can't get one. Well, I heard some young inexperienced fellows wanted to tackle it."

Then a smile came over George Gallion's face. He glanced up across the barbershop at his wife. Her face was strained.

"I could handle that school with one hand tied behind me," he said. "If they're the sons and daughters of the students I had, they're not outlaws. They've got good stuff in 'em."

"George, you couldn't be thinking about taking over that school," his wife interrupted. "You must think of your own health. Remember your last two years!"

"No, I'm not thinking about going back," he told her. "Only about what I would do if I were there. I can't forget what Ken said about no one seeming to care what goes on. I'm thinking about the fine kids I taught there. I haven't forgotten many faces. This shouldn't happen to those people. When I went there it was as rough as you said it is now. I had teachers who were as interested as I was. We changed that school until it was one of the best. Now, from what you say it's gone back to the jungle again."

"Professor," Ken said, waving his buzzing clippers, "I've told them down there they need you back. You remember when I kept running away from school and you told me if I did it again, you'd use the board of education on me? I wanted you to expel me. You told me you'd make that decision. Well, I tried you again, and honest, when you got through with me I looked to see if flames were shooting from the seat of my pants. Boy, I hated you for a while, and then the hate died. After you left, what happened? I walked out when I wanted to. I got kicked out. Then, Dad would see that I went back. But I got expelled for a double amount next time. Then I got so far behind I drifted out of school. Later I learned about discipline in the Army. It was some shock too!"

"I agree with you, Ken, we must have discipline," said the big man who was standing near the window. "I think that's the main trouble down at Kensington. Our young people down there are growing up like uncultivated corn. Put corn in the same field and cultivate one half and let the other half go and see the results. Kensington High School right now is the part of the field that was planted and not cultivated."

"The Professor could handle the situation even if he has been sick," Ken said. He raced his electric clippers up the other temple. "Yes, he can handle the place with a hand tied behind him!"

"Who are the young fellows wanting to be principal?" George Gallion asked.

"One is Harvey Winthrow," Ken said.

"I remember Harvey," George Gallion said. "He could never make up his mind. A man's got to work fast on a lot of small decisions in a big school. He's not the man. I taught him and I know. He'd make a good classroom teacher."

"Little Tommie Fillis wants it, and he qualifies," Tad said. "He got a big master's degree in college. He's a well-eddicated dood."

"I remember him too." George Gallion smiled. "When he ran away from school, I went to his home and he was hiding in the clothespress. I pulled him out and took him back to school. He never ran away again. But he won't make a principal of Kensington High School. He's too young and not a good enough student to work with veteran teachers."

"George, why are you so interested in who takes it?" his wife asked.

"Because I like school problems." He avoided her eyes.

"George, you don't think anybody can handle Kensington High School but you! Times have changed and the world is not like it used to be. You're thinking back twenty years ago! You were a young man in good health when you took that school over."

"Yes, and you know why I took it over, Grace. They had trouble. They had a scandal that got into all the newspapers. The chips were down when I went there. A high school principal has got to like a problem or he should stay out of administrative work.

If he's a principal, he's going to have more problems, even with a little school, than the executive who heads a big business. His problems are with human lives. A principal is the hub of the wheel and his teachers are the spokes. He'd better be strong. He'd better make decisions. No, I'm not the only one who can handle Kensington High School! I do know the people there and . . ."

"You *used* to know them," she interrupted him.

"Even if I wanted to be principal of Kensington High School, I couldn't get it," he said. "I disciplined John Bennington, who's now Greenwood County Superintendent, when he was a teacher on my faculty. I used to treat him pretty rough about his not getting his reports in on time." George stopped a moment and then continued thoughtfully. "Now, I can tell you one of my students who could discipline the school. Banks Broadhurst can handle it. On the football field he fought for inches when he couldn't gain feet. He was a good student and he could make decisions and stand by them."

"They've tried to get him, Mr. Gallion," said the big man against the wall, "but too late. He'd signed a contract with some large school in Ohio to coach there next year. He asked for a release, but they wouldn't release him."

"I can understand that," George Gallion said.

"Ever discipline Broadhurst, Professor?" Ken asked.

He chuckled as he made the scissors sing over his customer's head.

"No, Ken," he said. "But I took him to college and gave him five dollars. That's all the money he ever got, and four years later he had a degree. He didn't have any help and he was from a broken home."

"How can you remember so many?" Ken said.

"Because I've always been interested in my boys," he replied. "I sometimes wish I could forget some of them, but I can't."

"Professor, I can cut your hair now," Tad said as his customer got down from the chair. Tad smiled and brushed the loose hair from his white coat. "It's been a long time since I cut the Professor's hair. Who's been cutting it for you, Professor?"

George Gallion pretended not to hear the question. When he started to climb up in Tad's barber chair, Grace got up to help him.

"No, I can make it all right." He climbed up awkwardly. "It's good to be in your chair again, Tad," he said, grinning. "Good to hear all this news about Kensington High School too, even if it is bad news."

"Well, we're telling you the truth," Ken said. "The high school situation is all they talk about in Kensington. This is July and they don't have a principal. They don't have a teachers. There's talk that the school won't open in September. If it does and if one of the young fellows I mentioned gets to be principal, you'll see classes all over the hillside and down on the banks of the Tiber River."

Tad clipped George's long graying hair. It fell in wisps onto his lap and down around the chair.

"How old are you now, Professor?" Tad asked, "if ye don't mind my asking?"

"Not at all," he replied. "I'm forty-nine. But I still can handle Kensington High School!"

"You don't have to go back to schoolwork, and you shouldn't," Grace said. "You're just able to get around, so why think about it?"

"I can't keep from thinking I'm needed," he told her. "I'm thinking perhaps too much money and soft living has caused all that trouble down there."

"Yes, half the lads at Kensington High School have cars now," Ken said. "They drive away when they want to and burn the rubber on the highways. Big problem there last year was parking space."

"Only the coach and one of our teachers had cars when I was there before," George told them.

"I told you the world had changed," Grace said. "Your ideas are too old, George."

"Character and discipline are never old. We've had these for five thousand years!"

"If I had known you were going to get all worked up in here over a problem . . ."

"You would have cut my hair at home," he interrupted.

George's mind flashed back to the times she had cut his hair when he was propped up in bed. He remembered, too, the first time she cut it his hair was nearly down to his shoulders. This was after the long weeks under the oxygen tent and flat on his back, not allowed to move.

"By this time, Mrs. Gallion, you should have learned to be a good barber," Tad said.

"She's next to you, Tad." George laughed. "She did a good job."

"I want him to guard his health, Mr. Meadowbrook," she said.

"Can't blame you for that."

Now Tad had finished with him. George got down from the chair slowly.

"A Tad Meadowbrook haircut," he said, looking into the mirror at himself. "This is like old times again. You used to give me courting haircuts that wooed my wife, Tad," he said, trying to joke the serious look off Grace's face. "That's how I got Grace. You gave me traveling haircuts, farming and teaching haircuts! You make people look better, Tad! You are a successful man in this world. You've done something!"

"Oh, thank you, Professor," he said, laughing. "Now, I want you to come back again soon. Come back and bring Mrs. Professor."

All the customers had gone from the shop except the big man who leaned against the window. He still stood there smiling. When he smiled, his lips parted like an unzipped billfold so everyone could count his missing front teeth.

"Mr. Gallion, I'd like to speak to you alone a minute before you leave," he said.

"All right, let's step outside," George told him.

While they moved outside, Grace went back to the car.

"I don't want your wife to hear what I am going to say," he said softly to George.

"I don't keep any secrets from Grace. You can speak in front of her."

"I'd better not. I know how she feels," he said, "and I can't blame her. I don't want to hurt you but I used to know you in Kensington. I sold insurance there in those days. Two of my brothers-in-law went to school to you. Remember the twins, Ned and Ted Taylor?"

"I thought I knew you," George said. "You're Orman Caudill!"

"I'm chairman of the Greenwood County board of education now," he explained, "and we're really up against something at Kensington High School. Honest, I don't know who we are going to get to handle the school. And if you are able, I'll go to the superintendent's office right now. You said John wouldn't accept you because you'd disciplined him when he taught for you. Last week he said he wished for a man like you to take the school over. We can't pay you what you might ask us. I know you've made big money, but if you are interested and have the health, would you consider taking the school over? I can sympathize with you. I've had a heart attack too and if I don't get somebody who can handle that school, I'm going to have another one."

"I've got a doctor and a wife who'll have to pass on me," George said, smiling. "Each has a vote, and I'll have one."

"Your wife will be against your going."

"My doctor will have the deciding vote," George said. "Maybe I did say too much in there. Maybe I bragged too soon about handling it with a hand tied behind me."

"Would you even consider going back?" he asked George.

"Yes, if my doctor will okay me."

"When can I have the word from your doctor?" Orman said.

"I'll phone him," George said. "I'll let you know this afternoon."

"I'm going to hurry down to the office and tell John," Orman said enthusiastically. "The board meets Monday night and we have to hire somebody. We're desperate."

"He wants you to take the principalship of Kensington High School," Grace said when George went to the car.

"Right."

"Are you going to do it, George?"

"If I can pass the physical," he told her. "I am needed and I'll go back."

"Two years ago, you know what happened. Only by a miracle of good doctors and people's prayers are you a living man. I'm your wife and I stood by your bedside. I remember you in the oxygen tent, forty-six days on your back. One year in bed. Then, this past year you've spent convalescing. I remember your first step, because the nurse and I helped you take it. You screamed and said pins and needles were sticking your feet. And now you're interested in this school, George—I know you! We made a mistake coming here. I should have cut your hair again. George, you can't go back."

"You're my wife, Grace, not my doctor."

"I'm against it from the start," she said. "This will finish you."

"Let's get to a phone," he said.

"We don't need the money, George; we have security. You won't live to enjoy it."

"I've heard security in this country until I'm sick of it," he replied sharply. "That's all I hear these days. Economic security, social security, psychological security! Enough to last us to the end of our days. I've never known of anybody starving to death, but I've known people to rust out because they were afraid to live."

"What salary did he offer you?"

"None. I never asked him. I'm needed."

"You're egotistical."

"Maybe I am. Let's drive over to the telephone exchange where I can put in a phone call."

Tears welled up in her eyes as she drove down the street. There was silence between them now. When George got out, she got out too while he called Dr. Charles Vinn of Toniron, Ohio.

"George, is the building all on one floor?" Dr. Vinn asked him.

"No, there are two stories."

There was a long silence on the line. "I think it would be all right if you don't climb stairs. It's obviously something you want to do very much. But remember you had a double infarct. I'm sixty-eight now and have had only three patients survive this. You have as much scar tissue on your heart as a man can have. Think you can handle a high school?"

"I believe I can," George said. "If I see I can't do it, I'll resign. But it's a challenge, Doc, and I'm needed."

"You have my okay and you won't have to take a physical there. I'll send my okay to your local doctor."

"Thank you, Dr. Vinn." He hung up the receiver. "Two in my favor," George said smiling. "I'm in, if the superintendent and school board will hire me."

"You're in," Grace said sadly. "I've been married to you seventeen years and I thought I knew you. All I have to say is, this country is hard up for high school principals when a man of your physical condition has to return." She was almost crying. "You are my husband and I love you. I hate to see something happen to you."

"You're so right when you said this country is hard up for principals. For schoolteachers, too," he said, taking her by the hand. They walked out of the exchange onto the street. "It's damned hard up. You won't find any shortage of men in the professions where the big money is."

She waited for him to get into the car. "They're smart. You're not. You're a do-gooder and you're going into something blindly. Everything is against you. What can you gain? You're going back to where you started twenty years ago."

"Maybe so," he said. "I'm trying to do something for the kids. I'm not trying to promote myself."

"Your doctor won't even permit you to drive a car, yet he allows you to accept principalship of a problem school! It doesn't make sense."

"I don't believe in that old theory a school has to get bad before it can get better," George said as Grace drove down Main Street. "I think the moral bottom can drop out and it can stay that way." But she didn't answer, so he sat in silence as she drove.

"Grace slammed on the brakes and the car jerked to a stop under a large elm by a parking meter. They were in front of the Greenwood County school superintendent's office, a now shabby building which was once the home of a prosperous undertaker. This headquarters of educational enlightenment for thousands of young Americans was the most dilapidated of all the public buildings in Greenwood County.

"Well, we're here," he said. "Are you going in with me?"

"You bet I am. I might have something to tell the superintendent and that snaggle-toothed board member that hung around up there in the barbershop."

When he stepped on the rickety porch and opened the door, she was beside him.

Afterword

BECAUSE OF changes in the world around them, our nation's schools have taken on more and more responsibility, in many cases replacing home, church, and other social agencies in shaping our children during their formative years. The lives of countless young Americans bear witness to the fact that the family has declined as the basic social unit and provider of role models. For many families, the church is no longer a spiritual leader and provider of models of hope for the present or the future. Out of necessity, therefore, our schools have assumed functions for which they are ill equipped. The results have been catastrophic, as our present crisis indicates. We have a population confused about identity, direction, meaning, and purpose.

Jesse Stuart understood these problems and wrote about them. That he came down squarely on the side of Jean Jacques Rousseau and education as natural development rather than cultural development may indicate an awareness on his part that such either/or distinctions are rhetorical traps, for culture cannot be divorced from nature any more than the soul or spirit can be divorced from the body. In either case the result is death. Stuart knew that the past (forms of past experience) cannot suffice for present experience but can and must *inform* present experience. He realized that form is to the artist as formula is to the scientist. In both cases, form or formula is the shape a thing takes. One can force new experience into an old container, or he can let the experience take shape from within, but in the history of the human race mind has evolved with body in such a way that what one knows through the mind he first knows through the body. Thus there can be no break with the past, no cultural being who is not first a natural being, as "Early Education," the first selection in *Jesse Stuart on Education*, would have us believe.

Known in circles of education as the "war for the canon," the current struggle over what will be taught in our schools is based upon inadequate assumptions about what and who we human beings are, about what education is as well as what it can and cannot do, about concepts of time we call past and present, and about modes of existence we call mind and body. Furthermore, because I do not have space here to develop the matter of inadequate assumptions in detail, I would like to introduce briefly three sources that, when read in tandem, clearly formulate what is wrong with our schools, even though none of them is specifically directed at problems of education.

I recommend beginning with John Kenneth Galbraith's *The New Industrial State*, a book about economics, business, and technology.[1] Galbraith does a convincing job of explaining how the individual has been absorbed or lost in the larger planning system, a system he calls the "technostructure." Even more revealing is his explanation of the extent to which education has been made to conform to the purposes of the technostructure. Galbraith tells us much about how and where we place our values, about the present state of education in America, and about how our society demands mechanical or machine-like performance from its members.

The second book to be read in the series of three is Carl Sagan's *Cosmos*, a book that remains controversial because Sagan is a scientist and some people continue to think being a scientist is tantamount to being an athiest. However, my reading of Sagan is quite different from that. I cannot read him without thinking of Jesse Stuart because of his environmental concerns, because of his sense of and reverence for the mysterious life of the cosmos that embraces us: "Every aspect of nature reveals a deep mystery and touches our sense of wonder and awe."[2] Like Jesse Stuart, he is aware that we are only a moment out of the past: "How ignorant we are of our own past! Inscriptions, papyruses, books time-bind the human species and permit us to hear those few voices and faint cries of our brothers and sisters, our ancestors. And—what a joy of recognition when we realize how like us they were!" (281).

I like Sagan because *Cosmos* is a book about human spirituality, because he recognizes that mechanical explanations of the cosmos are insufficient, and because in his view we are made to participate in the life of the cosmos in a way that neither ignores nor denies transcendent reality. *"We* speak for Earth," writes Sagan. "Our obligation to survive is owed not just to ourselves but also to that Cosmos, ancient and vast, from which we spring" (286). What could be more important to education than how each of us participates in the life of the cosmos? Why else did Mitchell Stuart carry young Jesse into field and forest for the child's education in the flora and fauna of the region? And why else did Stuart the teacher continue the practice years later with daughter Jessica Jane? Why else did teacher and writer Stuart use metaphors in which the growth of an individual human being is compared to the growth of a tree in a thicket or forest of trees?

The third book, and the most provocative one, is *The Reenchantment of the World* by Morris Berman. I recommend it because Berman, in focusing on what he calls transformations of the human mind, is anything but apologetic. He declares, "The fundamental issues confronted by any civilization in its history, or by any person in his or her life, are issues of *meaning."* [3] Our loss of meaning in either a philosophical or a religious sense, he contends, began in the scientific revolution. Before the sixteenth century, he argues, the individual belonged to and participated in an enchanted world. However, from the sixteenth century to the present, he says, disenchantment as a mode of consciousness has paralleled the development of science:

Scientific consciousness is alienated consciousness: there is no ecstatic merger with nature, but rather total separation from it. Subject and object are always seen in opposition to each other. I am not my experiences, and thus not really a part of the world around me. The logical end point of this world view is a feeling of total reification: everything is an object, alien, not-me; and I am ultimately an object too, an alienated "thing" in a world of other, equally meaningless things. This world is not of my own making; the cosmos cares nothing for me, and I do not really feel a sense of belonging to it. What I feel, in fact, is a sickness in the soul. (3)

The modern dilemma, our dilemma, writes Berman, is that we can neither go back to the animism or alchemy which informed pre-sixteenth century consciousness nor survive the disenchantment brought on by a scientific world view for very long. The only way out of our disenchantment, Berman believes, is reenchantment through cultivating some form of holistic or participating consciousness and a corresponding sociopolitical formation. In *The Reenchantment of the World*, Berman first discusses in detail the enchanted world view and the forces that caused it to collapse. However, more than half of the book is devoted to a discussion of the possibilities of reenchantment, the possibilities of making the cosmos ours once again.

In *The New Industrial State*, Galbraith both defines and accepts the conditions of our disenchantment; but Sagan, in *Cosmos*, defines the conditions while registering his reluctance to accept them. In contrast, in *The Reenchantment of the World*, Berman both defines the conditions of our disenchantment and refuses to accept them. Rather, he discusses the possibilities of reenchantment as a necessity if the human race is to survive for very long. As Berman explains, "For more than 99 percent of human history, the world was enchanted and man saw himself as an integral part of it" (1).

I hope that what all this has to do with Jesse Stuart is becoming clear. Whatever labels we use to describe people and their opinions, the problem is ultimately our disenchantment as Berman defines it. Once we can see our disenchantment clearly, we will have to ask the old questions again: What is education? Education for what? Education for whom? Once we can see our disenchantment clearly, the answers will be different—very different—from what they are now: as different as we will be.

Since I first visited Jesse Stuart's beloved W-Hollow in Greenup County, Kentucky, in the mid-fifties, each time I have returned I have always been aware that I was in an enchanted place. Further, when I first read Stuart's early poems in *Harvest of Youth*, and, perhaps more important, in *Man with a Bull-Tongue Plow*, I was impressed that I was reading a celebration of an enchanted existence. The same thing happened when I first read his early stories in such collections as *Head o' W-Hollow* and *Men of the Mountains*, when I read such early autobiographical works as *Beyond Dark Hills*, and when I read such early novels as *Trees of Heaven*. As I quickly came to realize, the date of the writing was what counted, not the date of publication, for only those things written early celebrate an enchanted world. Even *The Thread That Runs So True* is a celebration of education in a land of enchantment.

Although it has become commonplace among Stuart scholars to say that the quality and appeal of the Kentucky writer's work

fell off beginning in the fifties, and that the celebrator of enchantment therefore never gained his power, I prefer a different explanation. That something drastic happened is true, as "The School
Bell Rings Again," from *Mr. Gallion's School*, aptly demonstrates. I
refer the reader to my discussion of *Mr. Gallion's School* in this
collection, but I also point out that before Stuart published that
book he began working on a collection of satirical poems called
"Birdland's Golden Age," poems through which he tried to come
to terms with what he at the time called the "madness of the
world." That disenchantment caught up with Jesse Stuart around
the time of World War II is clear enough. That he shifted his focus
and his method is also clear. His diaries, journals, correspondence, and such unpublished manuscripts as "Birdland's Golden
Age" make clear that from the time of the fifties, increasingly, the
celebrator of a closed, enchanted world became apologist for an
open, absurd world.[4] Having celebrated his closed, enchanted
world as an alternative to the open, absurd one, he moved outward and into the latter, both in *The World of Jesse Stuart: Selected
Poems* (1975) and in *My World* (1975). This was conscious move-
ment on his part, and one needs to understand that to make sense
of the thin book titled *The Kingdom Within*, in which he returns
from the open, absurd world to the closed, enchanted one as a
dead man. For the most part, when it appeared *The Kingdom
Within* baffled the critics. Nevertheless, Richardson writes in
Jesse, his biography of Stuart: "The genesis of *The Kingdom Within*
goes back at least fifty-two years to Jesse's high school days, very
possibly to his Bible course with Dr. Hatton; for it was during that
period that he read and applied Luke 17:21 to himself, . . . The
author said as much when he declared, 'It stuck with me all my
life, and it's the forerunner of *The Kingdom Within*.'"[5]

From the time of publication of his spiritual autobiography *The
Kingdom Within* in 1979 until his death in February of 1984, Stuart's
health declined rapidly. During that period his world was once
again the one he had described many years earlier in the prose of
Beyond Dark Hills, prose easily cast into lines because it has the
sweep of good poetry:

Call It God

Call it God, if you will.
The leafy trees in springtime,

the early meadows,
the old orchards
    white in apple-blossom time,
ridges of green Irish potato vines,
the blue streams
running between the dark hills,
the lonely sounds at night,
the wind in the oak tops
and the wind playing
    in the dead September corn
and running through the persimmon trees
on the broken pasture fields.
Rabbits in the dead weeds
and foxes barking
    from the ridge tops at night.
Call it God, if you will.[6]

Yes, Jesse Stuart came down early on the side of Jean Jacques Rousseau, believing that because man is a natural being, education must be a matter of natural development. He never changed his position, although he changed his focus and his method, as the selections in this volume indicate. All the money we can invest in education will make little difference if it is spent merely to deepen our disenchantment. More of the same thing will not suffice, and that is the problem with such writers as E.D. Hirsch, Jr., and Allan Bloom. We must have a bold, new beginning in which human consciousness is once again transformed. That is the challenge our schools face, as Jesse Stuart knew all along, and that is the task confronting every teacher, as Stuart never tired of saying: "[I] am firm in my belief that a teacher lives on and on through his students. I will live if my teaching is inspirational, good, and stands firm for good values and character training. . . . Good teaching is forever and the teacher is immortal."[7]

Too simple? Too idealistic? We have no choice. We must address the crisis in our schools.

Notes

1. I used the fourth edition of Galbraith's *The New Industrial State* (New York: New American Library, 1985), which is an authorized reprint of a hardcover edition by Houghton Mifflin.

2. *Cosmos* (New York: Ballantine Books, 1985), p. 275. For the curious reader I also recommend *Broca's Brain* and *The Dragons of Eden*, both by Sagan.

3. *The Reenchantment of the World* (New York: Bantam Books, 1985), p. 2. The Bantam edition contains the complete text of the hardcover edition printed by Cornell University Press in 1981.

4. For convincing evidence pertaining to this matter, see "Egypt and the World: Man of Letters 1960-1970," which constitutes chapter 16 of H. Edward Richardson's *Jesse: The Biography of an American Writer—Jesse Hilton Stuart* (New York: McGraw-Hill, 1984). Richardson discusses Stuart's Egyptian experience and his "Egyptian Diary" in detail.

5. See p. 446. See also pp. 442-47 of Richardson's *Jesse* for an excellent but brief discussion on *The Kingdom Within* as reenchantment. The context for Luke 17:21 is that of Christ's being questioned by the Pharisees about the coming of God's kingdom, and the verse reads: "Neither shall they say, Lo here! or, lo there! for, behold, the kingdom of God is within you."

6. See p. 183 of *Beyond Dark Hills* (New York: McGraw-Hill, 1972). *Beyond Dark Hills* was first published by E.P. Dutton in 1938.

7. See p. x of the preface in the 1958 Scribner edition of *The Thread That Runs So True*. *Thread* was originally published by Scribners in 1949.